# CONTEXT
# FOR DISCOVERY

## Into Our Third Century Series

# CONTEXT
# FOR DISCOVERY

## NEAL F. FISHER

## Alan K. Waltz, Editor

ABINGDON     Nashville

**Context for Discovery**

**Library of Congress Cataloging in Publication Data**

FISHER, NEAL F. (NEAL FLOYD), 1936-
  Context for discovery.
  (Into our third century)
  1.  Theology.  2.  Theology, Methodist.
  I.  Title.  II.  Series.
BT75.2.F57     230'.76     81-7929     AACR2

**ISBN 0-687-09620-0**

MANUFACTURED BY THE PARTHENON PRESS AT
NASHVILLE, TENNESSEE, UNITED STATES OF AMERICA

FOR

Kirk and Bryn

# Contents

# Foreword

In 1984, United Methodism will observe the 200th anniversary of the Christmas Conference of 1784—the date generally regarded as the beginning of the Methodist movement in the United States. We shall pause to remember how the Wesleyan vision of holy love and active piety spread like an unquenchable flame as the United States expanded from coast to coast; how people of all races, cultures, and classes rallied to a Gospel offering salvation and demanding good works as the fruit of Christian faith in God.

But we shall do more. Our bicentennial is also a time to soberly anticipate the future, to take stock of ourselves as we move into our third century. Our inheritance is rich in faith and works. It nourishes us, but our tasks are now, and tomorrow. The United Methodist Church is large (9.6 million members in the United States), still highly visible and active, but some indicators of our future prospects are disturbing. We shall reflect on and discuss these concerns as United Methodists, until we once again catch a vision of ministry and service that is worthy of our past, builds upon our present, and thrusts us again into the mainstream of human life with the message of God's redeeming love.

You, a United Methodist lay member or pastor, and your congregation have a vital role in both the celebration and the search. It is the people in the pews and pulpits of

United Methodism who must reestablish our identity and purpose, through discussion on who we are as United Methodists, what we wish to be and do, and how we will pursue our goals in the years ahead.

The Into Our Third Century series, initiated by the General Council on Ministries with the encouragement of the Council of Bishops, is intended to support your efforts. The series reports on extensive studies of selected issues of fundamental ministry and organizational concern to the denomination, and on studies of the environment in which United Methodism in the United States serves. Over a four-year period, beginning in 1980, seventeen separate volumes are being released for your use. The present book, *Context for Discovery*, is the eighth volume in the series. Other books already released are listed opposite the title page. Subsequent volumes will deal with the present realities and future form, content, and challenges of outreach ministry (mission, evangelism, and social witness), social movements and issues, ecumenical relationships, ethnic minority constituencies, professional ministry, roles of general agencies, financial support, and polity (the philosophy and form of church government).

The General Council on Ministries is pleased to commend to you this volume by Neal Fisher. This is a book about the relation of theology to life and the need to situate Christian faith in the midst of contemporary secularized living. It explores traditional United Methodist thought about the nature of our life together and the place of theology in United Methodist life and work. Dr. Fisher is writing to all of us—particularly those of us who are not specialists in theology. His is a serious effort to relate thinking to acting in the Church—and that we need.

Share your reflections within your own congregation, with other Christians, and with district, conference, and general church leaders. Your response will also be welcomed by the members and staff of the Council.

*Norman E. Dewire*
*General Secretary*

*Ezra Earl Jones*
*Editor*

*The General Council on Ministries*
*601 West Riverview Avenue*
*Dayton, Ohio 45406*

*September, 1981*

# Introduction

Early experience as a pastor convinced me that faithful witness in the world and sound theology belong together. I found frequently that individuals and congregations received added light on their faith only as they were willing to venture forth in a mission that employed the light that was already theirs. Put in different terms, it often appeared that Christians achieved clarity in the faith only in the heat of decisions, ventures, and risks that summoned forth the guidance, bearing, and hope that faith provides. Theological insight, I came to believe, was a consequence not only of clearer thinking, but of more intentional living and action. Theological convictions of the Church are contexts for discovering the deeper meanings of the Gospel.

In this book we attempt to build on these assumptions in examining what theology is and how it functions in the life of the Christian community. Our interest in this discussion is in the faithfulness and vitality of the whole Church, and we give particular attention to challenges faced by The United Methodist Church, and the heritage that is ours, in meeting those challenges.

In the first chapter, we shall attempt to describe what is at stake in the theological work of the Church. We shall contend that theological labors are not optional undertakings, but are the basic means for determining who we are, what we are to do, and what we have to proclaim to others. Our effort in addressing these foundation questions will not be to return to a bygone era in which the answers to fundamental questions were apparently clear. Neither shall we define the task as one in which we must strive to make the Christian message congenial to present-day assumptions. Rather, we shall argue that theological vitality requires critical engagement between the ancient witness of Christian faith and the contemporary experience of the believer, so that the one interprets and illuminates the other.

A second chapter will examine some of the challenges that confront theology today. We shall review some of the familiar arguments against belief, particularly those nineteenth-century challenges that have become part of the unexamined assumptions of many of our contemporaries. Our emphasis, however, will weigh more heavily upon a kind of practical atheism that, while not always explicitly challenging belief, nevertheless erodes and undercuts its foundations.

Having examined these challenges, we shall turn our attention to the manner in which theology functions in the everyday life of the believer. We shall seek to show that the roots of sound theology are a certain pattern of life and a certain style of discipleship. Theology, as it is described here, is embodied when it forms the context for discovering in our own experience the meaning of the realities testified to by Scripture.

In chapter 4, we shall focus upon the elements in a person's life that go together to make up one's theological point of view. We shall contend that our lives are shaped largely by (1) a way of perceiving or making sense out of the world we experience, (2) stories and images by which we select what we will give our attention to and how we will interpret it, (3) theories that integrate all of our experience into some intelligible whole, and (4) rituals and actions that represent, in a manageable form, what we understand life to be. These elements will be related to the three-fold division of human activities: thinking, willing, and feeling. The purpose of the discussion at that point will be to outline the way the vital forces of the whole person are involved in forming one's theological perspective.

Chapter 5 will single out some of the distinctive theological themes in United Methodist tradition that may support our efforts to think theologically in the future. The chapter notes the manner in which, from generation to generation, theological issues change in form even while the underlying human needs and hungers remain the same. We shall give particular attention to the four-fold standard embraced in the United Methodist tradition for discerning what God is saying to us in our own day.

A concluding chapter will examine particular qualities that will be necessary in the theological labors of all Christians in the time immediately ahead. We shall note the importance of our situation in life for the shape our theology will assume. We shall contend that theological vitality for the future will require a Church that is itself pluralistic and thus capable of interacting with, and learning from, a world whose experience is decidedly different from the experience of large numbers of United Methodists in the United States. We shall hold that it is in the context of aligning our lives with the purposes of God in our history that we learn to speak of God with clarity and conviction.

I am deeply mindful of debts owed to parishioners I have worked with, as well as to theological students in classes in which many of these matters were discussed. Colleagues on the faculty at Garrett-Evangelical Theological Seminary have offered encouragement as some of these topics were presented to them for discussion. I also wish to acknowledge the contribution of United Methodists in selected congregations who, in the months before this book was written, met with me and discussed the manner in which their own faith and theology were formed. To these persons, and the pastors who convened and participated in the sessions, I particularly express my gratitude:

## Acknowledgements

Christ United Methodist Church
Wellesley, Massachusetts
Dr. William C. Coleman, Pastor

Memorial United Methodist Church
Richmond, Virginia
The Rev. William R. Withers, Pastor

Simpson United Methodist Church
Arvada, Colorado
The Rev. Hidemi Ito, Pastor

St. Mark United Methodist Church
Chicago, Illinois
Dr. Maceo D. Pembroke, Pastor

Travis Park United Methodist Church
San Antonio, Texas
The Rev. Daniel E. Bonner, Jr., Minister

Since this project was written in the midst of a family move and a change in my position, my wife, Ila, shouldered more than her share of the family business so that the work could proceed. She also contributed critical judgments and encouragement at important points. We have inscribed this book to two young United Methodists from our home, in whom we place much hope.

# CHAPTER 1

# The Difference Theology Makes

## A. What Theology Is

When we use the word "theology," we mean, in the broadest sense, our speech about God. Used in this sense, theology is not an abstract academic language, reserved for those with an interest in such things; it is very much a part of the common speech of human beings. It is true that theology can become quite removed from the day-to-day interests of people, focusing on fine points of doctrines that are cared about, or understood, only by those who specialize in the study of such subjects. But theology as our speech about God is much more closely related to our everyday concerns than that. God is not an object of thought separate from life. Rather, "God" is the name given to that in life that is of absolute importance and concern to us. Martin Luther spoke of God in these terms:

> What is it to have a god, or what is God? . . . As I have often said, the confidence and faith of the heart alone make both God and an idol. . . . For the two, faith and God, have inevitable connection. Now, I say whatever your heart clings to and confides in, that is really your God.[1]

A more contemporary voice has called theology the discussion of "what concerns us ultimately."[2] In either definition, it is evident that when we speak of theology, we are not devoting ourselves strictly to an academic specialty, but to the basic human way in which we speak about what

17

in life finally matters to us. Put in this way, every person—whether consciously or not—is a theologian, for every person has some concern about life that is his or her final, or ultimate, concern.

In defining theology in this manner, we are purposely focusing on the way theology actually functions in the lives of people, rather than on a body of abstract and speculative ideas that is defended as the truth of Christian faith. This latter form of theology has an appropriate place, but it is not the form of theology that we are to consider here. Likely it is this more abstract form of theology that many people have in mind when they express indifference toward theology. Some consider it an academic undertaking quite separate from, or even in opposition to, the heartfelt faith present in the believer. Putting their emphasis on direct experience of God, many would hold that, for the one who has encountered God, theology is unnecessary; and for the one who has not had such an encounter, it is woefully insufficient.

Others have grown suspicious of theology because they regard it as a diversion from the real work of ministry to individuals and in society. Holding that the Church should simply preach the gospel and minister to human need, any speculation about abstract matters, such persons believe, is an escape from the obvious mandate for the Church.

But in this discussion we focus on the form of theology that no one can escape, for virtually any person who is serious about life speaks of some being, some center of value, some cause, some center of ultimate concern. Any reflective person "clings to and confides in" something in order to give life meaning and significance. In this broadest form, when we speak of such forces in our lives, we are engaged in some form of theology.

Conversations with numerous United Methodists have confirmed that persons in widely differing settings with highly diverse backgrounds did reflect theologically about their lives. Most United Methodists I spoke with in this study could identify critical events in which they believe that they have encountered, or have been encountered by, God. Often these experiences were in moments when they were in the extremities of life—whether in desperate sorrow or joy—and they came to interpret their lives within the context of God's presence and care. In the congregations I visited in preparation for this study, I found numerous persons who spoke of God in the context of an experience of deep suffering or of abounding joy, a desperate illness that threatened life, the loss of a close relative, the birth of a child, a critical career decision— these and a number of other experiences marked the times in which most people believe that they have experienced the presence of God.

But if theology is an indispensable element in the life of any serious person, it is also indispensable for the life of any church or denomination, including The United Methodist Church. As we, as United Methodists, anticipate the beginning of our third century in North America, it is an appropriate time to consider our theological bearings and their role in the concerns of The United Methodist Church. There are three practical functions that theological reflection ought to serve for the denomination. Theological reflection ought to help provide some identity for United Methodists. It ought to provide some practical guidance for the work of the church. And it ought to help shape the message that could be preached, in winning terms, to persons who are not now believers. In summary, three of the prominent theological concerns for United Methodists are *identity, guidance,* and *witness.*

### B. Prominent Theological Concerns of United Methodists

1. *Identity.* Louis Harris and Associates, an organization that studies public opinion, has recently confirmed what

United Methodists have long sensed: there is not a definite picture in the minds of persons inside or outside The United Methodist Church about its distinctive qualities. The Harris study showed that persons who are not United Methodists are generally neutral toward the denomination. They view it neither as particularly progressive nor as reactionary.[3]

The General Council on Ministries, a body representing every conference and each major constituency in The United Methodist Church, identified as one of the emerging issues in the four years before the 1980 General Conference the matter of our identity and purpose as a people of God. "Members are not clear," says the study, "what brings us together as United Methodists in the name of Christ." The group continued in its report to note the lack of a clear purpose around which the denomination can rally.

When *The United Methodist Reporter,* a church newspaper with a wide national circulation, expressed an editorial opinion that The United Methodist Church lacked a basic identity and spiritual direction, more than 1,000 persons responded to the questionnaire included for reader response. Large numbers of the responses referred to the need for more focus upon biblical authority and a need to reaffirm the basic principles of Wesleyan theology (though not generally advocating a narrow creedal authority). Frequent references were made to the need to center the life of the whole church in Christ and to transcend the preoccupation with what many felt were comparatively trivial internal concerns.[4]

It should go without saying that the question of identity is experienced by many members of ethnic minority churches in quite a different manner than it is by other United Methodists. Certain forms of identity questions may be distinctively white and middle- or upper middle-class in nature. Yet there are indications that the question of identity is as significant to ethnic minority persons as it is to other United Methodists.

A closer look at the question of identity suggests some of the individual elements that shape it. Concern about identity in The United Methodist Church clearly refers to *purpose* for the church—or a lack of it. In the times of flourishing numbers and swelling treasuries, it was possible to function on the easy assumption that everyone knew the purpose of the church, or, more likely, that there were enough resources to satisfy competing understandings of purpose. People were not often called upon to sacrifice what they considered essential in the functioning of the church. Such evasion of the basic questions of purpose is much more difficult, however, in a situation in which there is declining membership in many sectors of the denomination, and in which contributions, while increasing in nominal amounts, are actually declining in their purchasing power.

When it is clear that The United Methodist Church will not be able to do everything that all constituencies within the denomination believe is essential, the question of purpose becomes a critical one. Is the church to be essentially a *sanctuary*, a place where individual converts are gathered and schooled in the Christian life? Or is the church basically to be a *sign*, a demonstration, in and before the world, of God's saving purposes as they are manifest in advocacy and deeds for social justice? Is the church's primary work the worship of God through liturgical occasions, or is it acts of mercy and compassion outside the walls of the church? If someone protests that we cannot separate the individual and the social, the evangelistic and the prophetic, then on what basis and with what relative emphasis are they interconnected?

If theology is speech about God, then it is clear that answers to these questions are, in a significant way, theological answers. To know what the church is to do, and before what purpose or purposes it is to gather, is to make claims about what God is intending and accomplishing in the midst of historical happenings. Only by reference to that larger, more inclusive story, is there a possibility for refining an understanding of the purpose of the church within God's deeds among humankind.

The problem of identity is also expressed in the quest for the distinctiveness or uniqueness of being a United Methodist. In searching for an identity, we look both for what we share with others and for what is uniquely our own.

For some denominations this is much easier than it is for The United Methodist Church. Some denominations, for example, hold that the essence of Christian faith can be stated in propositions or creeds, which persons must affirm if they are to enter, or to continue in, church membership. In the book containing the law of The United Methodist Church, *The Book of Discipline,* there are "landmark documents," such as the Articles of Religion of 1784, but the Discipline makes it clear that these are legacies to be received in freedom, and are to be interpreted in the light of the historical circumstances in which they were first listed, rather than accepted in a literal way.[5]

Far from requiring adherence to certain literally interpreted creeds, the Discipline views diversity and pluralism as signs of strength rather than weakness.[6] Rather than prescribing a new creed for all to affirm, the Discipline invites all segments of The United Methodist Church to enter into the work of theological reflection.[7]

The identity of former generations of United Methodists was found primarily in their understanding of themselves as those who had felt the conviction of sin and had responded to the proclamation of God's grace. They identified the work of God's Spirit as the divine force in their lives leading them to repentance, redeeming them from their bondage to sin, and upholding and guiding them in a new life. Now, despite the fact that most United Methodists believe in such divine action, there is more diversity in the manner in which persons came to belief. By no means all, or even most, United Methodists can point to a single profound experience as the foundation for their Christian lives. And this diversity once again raises the question of the identity of the denomination as it enters its third century in America.

2. *Guidance*. A second concern of theology is its usefulness in guiding the work of the church. Of what practical guidance are the theological convictions of the church as it confronts a world marked both by soaring aspirations and by an insane rush toward self-destruction?

There are reasons to be somewhat modest in replying to the question. A General Council on Ministries report, to which we have referred above, comments upon our lack of a wide consensus on social issues and our lack of a commitment to address them through the church. The report of the laity to the 1980 General Conference, "The Long Journey: Laity in The United Methodist Church," likewise voiced concern about the inability of the church to act decisively on some of the most pressing questions facing humankind.

Citing the threats posed against the welfare and survival of the human race by persistent and growing starvation, pollution of the environment, and racism and other forms of oppression, the laity report questioned the ability of the denomination to respond to these issues.

Is The United Methodist Church alienated, separated from the society in which it exists to such an extent that it cannot see the human condition? Is the distance too great? Or, is The United Methodist Church so closely identified with that society that in its closeness it cannot see any difference? Is the distance too small?

The theological question implicit in the laity report's inquiry concerns the *identity* and the *relevance* of the church.[8] A church might be able to identify itself through its faith, and yet be so removed from people's suffering that it could not heed or hear them. On the other hand, the church in question might be so unclear about any distinctive identity and so accommodated to its social situation that it would come to view the interests of the dominant society and those of the church as essentially one. The prevailing temptation of the church is to identify Christian faith with the conventional beliefs and attitudes around it, thus abandoning any opportunity to offer any guidance.

Heinrich Ott, a Swiss theologian, tells of a conversation occurring in one of Bertolt Brecht's stories:

> Someone once asked Herr K. if there was a God. Herr K. said: "My advice to you is to think whether your conduct would change in accordance with the answer to that question. If it did not change then the question could be set aside. If it were to change, then I could help you at least by saying you have already decided: you need a God."[9]

It is a fair question to ask ourselves: Of what practical guidance is our belief in the reality of God? Under what mandates do we live because of our profession of faith in Jesus Christ? It is humbling to recognize the ways the Church has often reflected its surroundings rather than its grounding in the Word of God. Any sensitive Christian must shudder when he or she is reminded that large numbers of persons who bore the name of Christ justified the institution of slavery itself by quotes from the Bible. Was the question of God of any importance to them when it had so little capacity to overcome the conventional beliefs around them?

Yet what is even more humbling to us today is our seeming inability to register a strong, unified voice in

witness and action before some of the contemporary
equivalents of slavery. We find ourselves, for example, in
the midst of a costly and menacing arms race. It is hard to
imagine that this race, if continued, could end in anything
other than the indiscriminate slaughter of the human race.
In spite of our will to repress such a horrifying prospect,
most people are at least marginally aware of the
devastation our nuclear preparations entail. In one
California poll, 84 percent of the persons interviewed said
that nuclear war was likely and that they would not survive
it.[10]

Our interest at the moment is not to hold that all
Christians ought to find agreement on a policy to
recommend in the face of such an unimaginable peril. Our
suggestion is rather that our faith in God ought to provide
us with some basis for addressing the question in a way that
does not simply reflect the prevailing views of our social
group, our wage bracket, or our political party. If our
theological perspective provides us with no such guidance,
then can we really be said to have a theological perspective
at all?

It is at this point that the questions of identity and
guidance are so closely linked. For if we have no *identity*
that enables us to be different in the least from our
surroundings, do we in fact find any *guidance* from our
faith for the way we ought to go? One theologian put it
succinctly: "Only someone who finds the courage to be
different from others can ultimately exist for 'others,' for
otherwise he exists only with those who are like him. And
this is not much help to them."[11]

It is true that we who are United Methodists have
suffered an unusual temptation to accommodate ourselves
to our surroundings, since, for so much of our history, we
have been so thoroughly representative of the people of
the United States. President Theodore Roosevelt once said
that he never felt like he was with Americans so much as

when he spoke to a group of Methodists.[12] The fact that we were, until recently, the largest Protestant body in the United States, and even now remain the most thoroughly dispersed denomination, makes us representative of the nation as a whole in a manner different from most other church bodies. So long as there was a broad consensus in the nation on basic values and on principal ways of working on the issues of the society, it was tempting simply to reflect the consensus and identify it with Christian faith. Now, however, there is no similar consensus. This very fact will force the church in future years to come to positions on critical questions that, in the nature of the case, will provoke disagreement and dissension. The very presence of disagreement and diversity may force us to become much clearer about the biblical and theological basis for our actions as a church. If that is the case, then the matter of our theology will be an intensely practical question of guidance and decision, rather than simply an abstract or academic concern.

3. *Witness.* In addition to matters of identity and practical guidance, the matter of our theological conviction is significant for us in the communication of the faith itself. Without some clarity about what we believe about Christian faith, we can scarcely expect to commend it winsomely to others.

The most obvious measure of the problem before us is the oft-mentioned phenomenon of decreasing membership. Membership in United Methodist Churches decreased by 10 percent between 1970 and 1978. Church school enrollment decreased from 5.9 million in 1970-71 to 4.6 million in 1977.[13] There were 3,106 fewer United Methodist congregations in 1978 than in 1968.[14]

There are, of course, a number of reasons for this alarming decline, but these statistics at least provide a reminder that we are not commending the Gospel in a manner that prompts people to make the Christian faith their own. Can we really be said to have appropriated the Gospel if we cannot commend it meaningfully to others? In mastering a new word in our vocabulary, we are usually said to understand the word, to have grasped its meaning, when we can use it meaningfully in a sentence. To use a word in a sentence signifies that we have understood its linkages with other words, its relationship to a context, and its place in a sensible chain of thought. In some parallel fashion, to have appropriated Christian faith requires that one not only be able to articulate its formal meanings, but also be able to phrase it within the context of everyday life. If we fully grasp its meaning for us, then we should be able to phrase it in such a way that it has a clear connection with the other aspects of our life.

The evangelistic task of the Church is admittedly more difficult when symbols of the Christian faith are used so pervasively. The very frequency with which the name of God is involved in political discussion, for example, make it difficult to recover the full force of that term in human experience. It is doubtless more difficult to speak of Christian faith in our culture than it would be in a land where the name of Christ was scarcely heard.

But having admitted these difficulties, United Methodists can hardly be complacent in the face of our lack of effectiveness in commending Christian faith. Our origin and history are in a movement organized for the purpose of converting individuals and transforming communitites. The standard for admission into the early Wesleyan societies was not doctrinal conformity but an intent about one's life. Said John Wesley, "There is one only condition previously required in those who desire admission into these Societies, *a desire to flee from the wrath to come, to be saved from their sins.*"[15]

"Orthodoxy," he wrote elsewhere, "or right opinions, is, at best, but a very slender part of religion, if it can be

allowed to be any part of it at all."[16] This was not, of course,
because Wesley was indifferent to the contents of Christian
teaching; indeed, he spoke out against the "latitudin-
arianism" of those who were perpetually unsettled in their
thinking, driven to and fro by every teaching.[17] But even
the matter of Christian doctrine itself, important as it was
to Wesley, was subordinated to the mission of bringing
men and women to the point of radical transformation and
change that was the mark of God's Spirit working in their
lives. It was the goal of the Methodist societies to spread
scriptural holiness throughout the land. The origins of
Methodism are in an aggressive movement, organized
around the task of personal and social transformation.

It is a theological concern of some magnitude to
articulate Christian faith in such a way that it connects
meaningfully with the lives of people today. As we shall
discuss in later chapters, we are at a critical turning point in
our history. If humankind is to survive in any meaningful
form on the face of this planet, we must undergo some
fundamental shifts in our understanding of ourselves, our
fellow creatures, and how we are to interact.

Threats to human survival are well known—exhaustion
of nonrenewable resources, pollution of the atmosphere,
upsetting of precarious balances in our environment, or
the outbreak of cataclysmic war. It would be tragic indeed
if, at such a turn in history, a movement such as The
United Methodist Church, founded with a sense of
urgency and mission, were now to fail to provide any
meaningful declaration of the Word. In the late 1950s,
James Broughton mocked our society and its inability to
declare a meaningful word in the face of such threats to
human life, in his short play, "The Last Word." It is set in
the Last Chance Bar on the night the bomb is to fall. A
couple named Rusty and Dusty Augenblick (German for
"moment" or "instant") are saying their last words to each
other before the end comes. They recall that they forgot to

collect the laundry or put out the garbage. But they themselves are stunned that they have so little to say in the face of such an enormous tragedy. "Why can't we think of anything to say?" Dusty says to Rusty. And again she inquires, "Have we anything to declare?"

At last the bomb falls, and they, having discovered nothing to say, recite their secular liturgy:

DUSTY:  It's cold in here.
RUSTY:  United Nations, have mercy upon us!
DUSTY:  Elizabeth Arden, deliver us!
RUSTY:  General Motors, have mercy upon us!
DUSTY:  Sigmund Freud, deliver us!
RUSTY:  Batten, Barton, Durstine and Osborn, have mercy upon us!
DUSTY:  In the name of Mutual Life and Cold Storage.
RUSTY:  Amen.
*Silence.*[18]

It is a matter of some theological concern that the Church have something meaningful to declare, not only at the last hour, but at every hour until that time. To phrase the message of the Gospel as it intersects the concerns of persons today is a theological undertaking. It requires a sensitive reading of the story of God's dealings with people in the past, and an engagement with events in our history as they are illuminated by the biblical witness.

## C. The Way Ahead

To this point, we have sought to show that the question of theology among United Methodists is a profoundly practical concern for the church and its mission. There are many wonders to be wrought by technology, and we would not for a moment want to sacrifice the humanitarian advances technology has made possible. But the basic questions bearing upon human survival are those technology cannot answer: What is the "good life"? What is our responsibility to our environment? What are the claims of justice at this juncture of human history? How do we find the sources of the transformation that is necessary in our personal and our corporate life? These questions are fundamentally theological.

But, having made this claim, out of what stance are we to address these theological questions? There are three positions Christians frequently take in seeking to relate faith and contemporary life. In this section we shall look briefly at each of the three and suggest the one that will be most useful for the discussion in the following chapters. The three positions may be designated as *reaction, accommodation,* and *critical engagement.*[19]

1. *Reaction.* The stance promoted by many Christians is one oriented to historic doctrines and affirmations. Such persons hold that the Church will find theological integrity and effectiveness in its mission when it repudiates the secularity that has crept into our modern world-view, and returns to the perspectives of the Bible and the teachings of earlier generations. To become a Christian, according to this perspective, is to replace with a biblical view of the world, some prevailing notions about the world that are held by our contemporaries. Persons representing this stance frequently place a high premium on the Christian community. Such an emphasis helps to confirm a world-view among a tightly knit body of believers that is at some variance with the world-view of others with whom they associate.

Persons who embrace this option for meeting the theological needs of the day frequently present one doctrine or a set of doctrines as definitive for all scriptures. In earlier days there was a set of "fundamentals" that all true adherents were expected to embrace, and those fundamentals (such as the Virgin Birth, blood atonement, bodily resurrection, etc.) were said to constitute the non-negotiable elements of Christian faith. Others may emphasize certain experiences attested to by scripture and tradition as determinative for Christian faith. Frequently there is a prescribed conversion experience, based on testimony from Christian history, an experience of speaking in tongues, or some other form of the work of the Holy Spirit in one's life.

What is significant in all of these positions is that the theological answer that is proposed for our situation is some teaching or some experience that is found in the past. That way of thinking or feeling is recommended as a source of meaning, integrity, and salvation that is thought to replace the conventional views and perspectives of modernity.

2. *Accommodation.* Another prevalent response to the current situation is to focus on some aspect of the *present* situation rather than on the past. In this response, some contemporary thought form or project is made the authoritative perspective from which any historic tradition is to be appraised and verified.

Persons of distinctly different theological positions adopt this posture. Some have embraced a program of social change and have made the progress of that movement the final criterion for any theology. Some—though by no means all—of the contemporary movements for liberation will view economic and social transformation as the goal, with historic Christian faith as a means to that end. Others, from a quite different social position, assume that Christian faith is primarily an endorsement of certain prevailing or prospective values, and these values themselves become the measure for Christian faith. Thus, "the American way of life," "free enterprise," community stability, patriotism, productivity, or a number of other, similar values may be introduced as the basis for Christian faith, and the Christian message is embraced as a bulwark for values that arose quite independently of that faith.

In yet another accommodative response, Christian faith

may be commended to others as the basis of personal fulfillment, success in love or business, or as an asset for achieving any of a number of personal desires. In this form, being Christian is recommended on the basis of its value for good mental health, an optimistic view of life, physical health, higher income, or a number of other desired ends.

In contrast to the reactionary's assumption that the historic formulation of our faith is authoritative, the accommodative response tacitly assumes that whatever is modern is, by virtue of being modern, superior. This position appeals to the norms of contemporary discussion as the standards by which all previous positions are to be evaluated. If Christian faith clashes with the contemporary scientific world-view, for example, then it is assumed that those elements of faith that create the conflict must be eliminated. Seldom are the assumptions behind contemporary views challenged. On the other hand, the accommodative position frequently attempts to commend Christian faith on the basis of the testimony of contemporary thought. Thus, when some form of current science announces a finding that tends to corroborate Christian faith or to allow an opening for Christian faith, this finding is taken as a signal permitting or authorizing belief. For example, some medical testimonies of those who have been clinically dead and returned to life are assumed to substantiate, or at least allow for, Christian faith in everlasting life. What is common to the accommodative response is that some form of contemporary experience is viewed as the mountaintop, the standard of measurement, by which and from which all human thought and experience should be evaluated. For the reactionary, all authority is vested in the past; for the accommodative response, the present is the measure of all things.

3. *Critical Engagement.* Neither of these positions, at least in their purer forms, represents a very adequate response

to the theological challenges now before the Church. To confine God's self-disclosure to the past tends to lead us to view God as a historical relic, once active, but no more to be reckoned with. On the other hand, to make Christian faith an instrument for realizing some value in the present, to measure everything by the contemporary mind, is obviously a form of idolatry. Some element of our own making is erected as the primary value, and all else—even God—is viewed as a means to that end.

Yet it is clear that both positions have a grasp on something essential. Even though we do not confine God's self-disclosure to the past, there are clearly special events, witnessed to in Scripture, which are of central significance for our understanding of God and the world. Yet, with the accommodative stance, we must agree that whatever comes to us out of the past must connect meaningfully with our present experience, or we could not even know its meaning. We, as human beings, cannot survey all life from the perspective of eternity; that belongs to God alone. Therefore, we have to gain such light as we can find *through*—not outside of—our contemporary experience. *Both* the past and the present must play a critical role in the theological reflection that is necessary today. We might label such a stance "critical engagement." We are using the word *critical,* emphasizing its root meaning of judgment and decision. Theological inquiry, as we are viewing it, is not an automatic acceptance either of past authority or of currently prevailing norms. It is an act of judgment and decision, a venture of discovery, in which persons and communities connect historic faith and contemporary experience. "Engagement" is used to signify the inter-action in theology of the past and the present.

Emphasis of both past and present is, in our view, a more adequate expression of how people actually come to faith. Historic faith provides, for those who embrace it, the basic stories through which contemporary life is experienced.

When a person refers to some suffering as "a cross I'll have to bear," for example, that expression tells us much about how that person will confront suffering. By referring to suffering through the biblical story of the cross, that person has already decided to view suffering as redemptive and victorious, rather than as a meaningless and cruel experience. At the same time, it is in the present experience of suffering, the taunting of onlookers, the betrayal by friends, the experience of apparent abandonment, that we gain some glimpse of the meaning of the cross for Jesus. In this instance, present experience illuminates historic faith, and historic faith provides a way of viewing contemporary experience. *Engagement* refers to this interaction between the two.

A number of years ago, this interaction was expressed in the following terms:

> Doing theology is a dynamic process in which we reflect on our involvement, rekindle memory and hope and plan our strategy for shaping the future. We reflect on God's activity in past history, we look for signs of his activity in the present, we join his mission witnessing to his presence, we reflect on our experience as we clarify and interpret God's will and our tasks, and we move on to implement the tactics indicated. The theological process, therefore, implies a dynamic interplay between sensitizing oneself to faith history and participating in one's history with faith.[20]

As this statement implies, critical engagement involves an implicit commitment to the future as the place where God's self-disclosure is to be found. Through the history of God's deeds in the past, we are sensitized to the points at which God's work is to be found in our day. We are helped to recognize the presence of God in our history. We have used the word *discovery* to indicate that the presence of the living God is never to be *contained* in declarations from the past or in projects within the present. God is One who is always out ahead of us, even as God went before the people of Israel in cloud and fire, leading the way into the place of promise.

The stance of the believer today is neither to fix upon the past nor to follow each fad from the present. The believer is one who is a part of a community of expectancy. Scripture and tradition are authoritative because they help place one in the context of God's fuller self-disclosure. Scripture and tradition help to orient one. They serve as waymarkers on the path of discovery. Theology, therefore, rather than fixing primarily upon either the past or the present, embraces and engages both in a movement of faith toward the future.

In the present study, it is not assumed that theology itself will save the Church. Even less is it assumed that only professional theologians are to be entrusted with the mysteries of faith. Peter Berger, himself a lay person, quipped: "What the 'professional theologians' have done of late is not so inspiring that we unaccredited types must be constrained to stand watching in awed silence."[21] In this discussion we shall appeal for the involvement of every Christian, and specifically those who stand within the United Methodist tradition, to become involved in the work of participating in life with hope and reflecting upon hope in the light of the experience of life.

We shall discover in this discussion that theology is far more than an academic undertaking, though it includes rigorous thinking. It is a means by which our very identity is provided, the way we guide our actions, and the means through which we articulate and commend our witness to others. Theology is an interaction of action and reflection, of willing and feeling, that not only gives us information about the way things are, but points us in the way of faithfulness.

# CHAPTER 2

# CHALLENGES TO THEOLOGY TODAY

The challenge of relating historic faith and one's contemporary experience is not a new one. But there are distinctive ingredients in our current situation that at least present that challenge in new forms. In the following discussion, we shall look at some of the explicit challenges, as well as at some of the more pervasive and unexamined implicit challenges, that are posed for theology today.

## A. Arguments Against Belief

Religious belief primarily as assent to the truth of certain propositions is a Greek, rather than a biblical, notion. Most biblical mention of belief concerns trusting and relying on God with one's whole being, rather than merely assenting to a proposition about God's existence. There are none in the pages of the Old Testament who deny God or who advance arguments against the Divine Being's existence.[1] In the psalms that speak of the unbeliever (Ps. 53 and parallel in Ps. 14) such a person is called a fool:

> The fool says in his heart,
> 'There is no God.'
> They are corrupt, doing abominable iniquity;
> There is none that does good. (53:1)

In this psalm, the unbeliever is not so much one who

denies God as a theoretical reality, as one who acts as if God were not near. It might be translated:

> The fool says in his heart,
> 'God is not here.'[2]

This fool is immediately identified by his deeds. It is not merely his thought that is in error; it is a pattern of life, an attitude of practical atheism, with which the writer of the psalm is struggling. Belief, in this instance, is not merely a way of thinking but a whole orientation of life.

It was the Greek mind rather than the Hebrew that sought to go beyond the stories and myths of popular religion and to build a set of rationally defensible propositions about God and the world. To that end, a thinker such as Plato develops arguments for belief in the existence of God, immortality, and the integrity of the moral order. On the other hand, the questions that troubled the biblical authors were much more closely related to the whole enterprise of living a faithful life. They struggled with questions of faith in God as opposed to faith in the idols. They agonized over what forms of obedience this God required of them. These questions, rather than matters of the theoretical validity of their faith, vexed them.[3]

It will not serve the purposes of this discussion to outline all the subsequent forms arguments against belief have taken within the course of Western history. There are some signal developments in the nineteenth and twentieth centuries, however, that can hardly be ignored if we are to understand the contemporary context for theological belief. There are four theoretical objections to belief that, while in their strictest form are not embraced by a majority of persons, nonetheless form a part of the background for many of our contemporaries. Stated directly, they will help us understand some of the challenges confronted by theology today.[4]

1. *Theological belief detrimental to human freedom and dignity.* *Ludwig Feuerbach* (1804–1872) is a key figure in the arguments introduced against belief. It was his contention that God is entirely a human creation, a projection by human beings of attributes they find in themselves. This act of projection produces alienation. Humans come to think of God—really a projection of themselves—as something other, or alien from them. Then the object of their own making turns against its creators, and they become its predicate.[5]

Since God is human nature objectified by humans, reference to God as a distinct, superhuman being is a "false consciousness" and must be changed.[6] The appropriate action, therefore, is for humans to recognize themselves in the object they have created, to take back for themselves what has been attributed to God, and to redirect the love that was once directed to God to other human beings instead.[7] The "beginning, middle, and end of religion," said Feuerbach, "is MAN."[8]

The assertion that the idea of God is a human projection has been adopted by a large number of those who have argued against religious belief in subsequent history. The negative effects on human beings of this projection have been the underlying theme of modern atheism.[9] That is, the question of *whether* the idea of God is a human projection has not been debated; it has largely been assumed. The active question has been whether such an idea is an unessential and illusory one. The opposition of many to Christian belief has been on the grounds that the notion of God represents a misunderstanding on the part of humankind, one that will eventually disappear. Among them there has been agreement that humans do not need the aid of God. More than that, such a notion is an intrusion upon their freedom and dignity.

*Karl Marx* (1818–1883) embraced the notion that God was the projection of human beings, and he modified the notion of alienation that Feuerbach and Hegel, in widely different interpretations, had supported. Instead of focusing on the religious object, God, who is treated as alien, or other, Marx focused on the workers' alienation from the products they create.

It was less out of speculative disavowal of God than from the need for action that Marx rejected belief. He held that one must seek truth, not in an abstract realm, but in one's actual labor to produce and to transform society.[10] His famous eleventh thesis on Feuerbach puts it: "The philosophers have only interpreted the world in various ways; the point, however, is to change it."[11] Religion, however, provides a justification or sanction for this world as it is. The source of human alienation is in human social and economic relations. The state is the real agent responsible for this social reality leading to alienation. Religion is at once an expression of the alienation and a protest against it. "Religion is the sigh of the oppressed creature, the heart of a heartless world, just as it is the spirit of a spiritless situation. It is the *opium* of the people."[12] Religion drugs people with the expectation of an illusory happiness rather than a real happiness here on earth. Because religion participates in and justifies an oppressive situation, it must be abolished for the sake of human welfare. "The abolition of religion as the *illusory* happiness of the people is required for their *real* happiness. The call to give up illusions about its condition is the demand to give up a condition which needs illusions."[13] Religion is thus a symptom of a diseased society.

Joining with Feuerbach, Marx, and others in rejecting what he regarded as an injurious projection on the part of humans themselves is *Sigmund Freud* (1856–1939). Like them, he believed that he had discerned the origins of religion and rejected it on the grounds of its alleged ill effects upon people. For Freud, God was "nothing other than an exalted Father"; therefore, the qualities attributed to God are nothing but projections of childhood ideas of mother and father.[14]

Freud conjectured that the origin of the notion of God rests in the action of brothers who had driven out and killed their father, the male figure who had dominated them. Having killed their father, they devoured him. The ritual meal commemorates this, and the image of the killed and devoured father has been translated into deity. God remains a wishful illusion for human beings, an illusion they must be educated to surrender for their own maturity.[15] If they are helped to surrender religious illusions, they can then use the energy formerly devoted to those illusions to help make life tolerable for all and oppressive to none.[16] Continued reliance upon the illusions would only tend to hallow corrupt institutions and impoverish human intelligence by dulling critical thinking. Religion is a universal obsessional neurosis from which humanity needs to be relieved. Only by becoming free from the authority of God can humans cease being children and develop their full capacities.[17]

Freud theoretically granted that the illusory status of religious beliefs does not necessarily make them false; he and his followers profess not to be concerned with the truth or falsity of those beliefs. He did suggest, however, that the coincidence of our belief in God and our natural wishes for a moral order and a future life makes our belief highly suspect.[18] His own rejection of belief in God was quite explicit and emphatic.

Freud's present-day followers share his theoretical openness about the truth or falsity of religious beliefs, but they also share his conviction about their illusory character. The contemporary Freudian, Ana-Maria Rizzuto, for example, basically agrees with her mentor on the origins of belief in God. If she departs from Freud in his wish to educate people away from the illusion, it is not because she differs with him about calling belief illusory. It is only because she holds that "to ask a man to renounce a God he believes in may be as cruel and as meaningless as wrenching a child from his teddy bear so that he can grow up."[19]

Throughout Freudian thought, the search for meanings beyond human projection is regarded as a sign of sickness. The promised help is found in psychoanalysis. Through this therapy we are promised salvation from our neuroses, illusions, and complexes.

Joining with the authors mentioned here are a number of other prominent names in Western thought, including Nietzsche and Sartre, who would insist that belief in God is morally questionable, since it submits human choices and decisions to a norm not of their own creation and not under their control.[20] This helps make it possible for humans to avoid responsibility, and it elevates standards other than human welfare and well-being for human compliance. Faith in this context, say these authors, can be a flight from freedom.

2. *No trustworthy evidence to support theological belief.* In addition to these foundational arguments against theological belief, a number of other contentions are made in recent thought that deter some from belief in God. For the purposes of this discussion, these are noted briefly, but will not be elaborated.

It is often argued that belief in God is supported by no evidence of the sort deemed necessary for determining the truth in other fields of investigation. The only evidence cited by believers, goes this argument, is either founded on alleged divine revelation, or on the presupposition the believer brings to experience in the first place. In neither case does the belief have any independent standing. It is dependent solely upon the private assumptions of the individual.

The phenomena religious belief has been called upon to explain can be accounted for much more adequately in recent history by scientific accounts. The father of modern sociology, Auguste Comte (1798–1857) suggested that there are three stages through which human thought has passed: theological, metaphysical, and scientific. The first two stages were introduced to fill the gaps in knowledge that are progressively being filled by science. Science, therefore, is destined to eventually take over all the functions formerly served by religious beliefs.

3. *The experience of evil.* The problem of evil has always been a challenge to belief. But the magnitude of the threat that now hangs over the human race from evil and suffering is so significant in degree as to constitute a problem that is different in kind. In addition to the natural evil our forebears have experienced, contemporary human beings have been faced with the reality of death camps, hydrogen bombs, and an arms race, systemic and pervasive racism, napalm, and mass starvation in the face of plenty. If God is both great and good, how can such unspeakable suffering occur? In the face of such suffering, should we not call such a God more a demon than a redeemer?

4. *The term "God" has no clear and definite meaning.* Modern philosophy has given significant attention to the analysis of language and the study of its meaning. The fundamental challenge to Christian faith coming out of this study is, not that theological beliefs are untrue, but—much more seriously—"that they have no certain meaning."[21] Statements are classified into those that simply establish definitions and conventions in language (analytic statements), those that convey information about our feelings as individuals (emotive statements), and those that purportedly state facts about a real state of affairs (synthetic statements).[22] For any statement claiming to inform us about a real state of affairs, there must be a

definite means of verifying or disproving it. Verity and falsity are determined empirically. So long as religious believers can point to no set of circumstances that would either prove or disprove God's existence, belief in God is not even a meaningful proposition. Belief in God is only a statement of emotion, informing others about how we feel, or an analytic statement, establishing how we are going to define the term.[23]

More recently, some philosophers and theologians have held that there are different contexts for the use of language, and that the principle of verification cannot therefore be applied in the same way to each context. Yet even with these modifications in the verification principle, statements of religious belief are not said to convey information about a real state of affairs outside the mind of the person who is speaking. They serve rather as expressions of feeling or of intention to act in a certain way. Their effect is simply to convey information about the speaker rather than about the reality to which the speaker refers.

These arguments against religious belief have been summarized without comment. Our interest in this discussion is not to treat them as points of debate that are to be refuted. Rather, we are here viewing them as a part of the intellectual background of our present era. Our challenge in subsequent sections will be to outline an approach to theology that establishes its standing as an authentic response to an encounter with what is ultimately real.

### B. The Pervasiveness of Practical Atheism

Far more telling for most moderns than the theoretical arguments advanced against belief is the practical atheism that pervades contemporary life. Practical atheism is a term describing that style of life, that fundamental

disposition toward the world, which, without debating the
question, acts as if God were not present in life. The "fool"
in Psalm 53 was a practical atheist, for he said in his heart,
"God is not here."

Each cultural period maintains some pervasive assumptions about life, assumptions that are seldom challenged,
because we are rarely aware of them as matters for debate.
They are unspoken, and so accepted as a part of life. Until
recent years, our attitudes toward "rugged individualism,"
unlimited growth, and progress fell into this category.
Alfred North Whitehead was referring to this basic set of
assumptions when he said:

> When you are criticizing the philosophy of an epoch, do not
> chiefly direct your attention to those intellectual positions
> which the exponents feel it necessary explicitly to defend.
> There will be some fundamental assumptions which adherents
> of all the various systems within the epoch unconsciously
> presuppose. Such assumptions appear so obvious that people
> do not know what they are assuming because no other way of
> putting things has ever occurred to them.[24]

Such assumptions about the world are embedded in our
language. It is true that human beings form language, but
it is also true that, thereafter, the language has a formative
influence on how we think.[25] To take only one of the more
dramatic examples, many have discovered, only in recent
years, the assumptions about male superiority with which
our language is saturated. But in much more subtle ways,
our language selects for us what we will heed and what we
will respond to. It embodies a certain perspective that
colors all our perception. The fact that Eskimos have a
profusion of names for snow, each indicating a different
color and texture, and that Arabs can refer to camels with a
variety of names, indicates something about their daily
associations; but it also heightens their sensitivity to key
features of their environment. The world they live in is

changed by the more refined names by which they refer to prominent elements of their life.[26]

Karl Rahner has referred to the web of assumptions in our language and culture that influences the way we think as "latent heresy." Commenting on this term, Allen Dulles observes: "Many of the unspoken assumptions of our culture are out of harmony with Christian faith. Thus we imbibe from our environment a kind of 'latent' or 'implicit' heresy. . . . "[27]

We need to examine this web of assumptions and the forces acting on it if we are to assess the situation confronting theology in the church. In this discussion, we will examine some of the more prominent elements of those assumptions.

1. *Modernization and the Erosion of Plausibility Systems.* Peter Berger has provided one helpful way of addressing the changes in the web of assumptions and their impact upon belief by his phrase, "plausibility systems."[28] In using the term he is expressing his conviction as a sociologist that human beings require social agreement and support for the beliefs they hold about reality.[29] The four-year-old boy who falls on the sidewalk, scrapes his knee, and is effusively praised by mother and father for not crying, is receiving powerful confirmation about one's attitudes toward pain, emotion, and masculinity. Victims of brainwashing illustrate how one's whole world can assume drastically different shape simply by the repeated confirmation (and, in this case, rewards and punishment) of a certain perspective upon that world.

We all have deeply ingrained attitudes about our world and our role in it that are not derived from experience itself, though they are so fundamental and so widely shared that we tend to think them as obvious as the difference between up and down. We can see this most clearly in the contrasts between different cultures on fundamental notions of hospitality, on what constitutes compassion toward others and when it should be shown, on what foods are appropriate for human consumption, and the significance of death.

It should be added that whenever any of the plausibility structures are threatened, additional efforts must be invested in reaffirming and reconfirming them. When one loses a loved one, one's whole construction of the world and one's relationship to it is jeopardized. One can hear, in the halting and sometimes embarrassed comments of friends to the bereaved, an effort to place this calamitous loss in such a perspective that the world will still make sense for the one who has suffered the loss. Likewise, the ritual of worship is a powerful way of calling a person and a community to account before the faith it holds about Ultimate Reality, God, and of showing the way even death fits into a system, a system that is to be trusted and embraced. Ritual, as well as spontaneous conversation, provides a way of confirming the plausibility system.

In a stable society there is little threat to the plausibility structure. There are always some deviants, to be sure (the stubborn village atheist, the local knave, or the "kook"), but the stability of the plausibility system is reinforced by the nearly universal recognition that such persons in fact stand outside the consensus of the community, and are treated accordingly.

Berger has argued convincingly that a major element of modernization (and, as we shall see later, also an aspect of secularization) is the decline of the cohesive view of things, accompanied by fatalism and the multiplication of *choice*.[30] In earlier societies, there was little dispute about what training one should have, what occupation one should follow, how (or even whom!) one should marry, how the children should be reared, etc. Similarly, the religious symbols holding those societies together were well established, great bodies of assurance broken only here and there by a doubt or a differing opinion. Persons who lived in such a society could have reasonably firm assurance that God had ordained that life should be arranged as it was.

Such automatic assurance about what the world is like is not available for most persons today. There is no one pattern of life that is universally confirmed. One must choose. In such a situation, when the world no longer presents itself to an individual as an ordered whole, the natural inclination is to turn within oneself to one's own experience to find what assurance one can. It is natural, therefore, that we should be witnessing a greater emphasis on subjectivity. Great attention is devoted to "whatever turns you on" and leads to self-fulfillment. The magazine, *Self,* is only putting in its title what other magazines have long since recognized: people are going to read more avidly about their self-concerns (diets, appearance, sexuality, pleasure, exercise, possessions) than they are about issues in a larger world.

The force of modernization and the erosion of plausibility systems has, of course, made one's belief, like most other elements of one's life, a matter of choice. Each individual lives through a variety of plausibility structures as he or she participates in the office, factory, school, suburban party, church, lodge, office party, or any other setting in his or her work week. Whereas one could formerly adopt the prevailing consensus about the world, in a time in which there is no such consensus, one must choose.[31]

In such circumstances, pluralism in the society and within a denomination will be an unavoidable fact, whether applauded or scorned. Since no one form of belief is going to have the social force behind it that the consensus formerly commanded, persons who are converted to a faith are going to be converted because they have been persuaded that its efficacy for their lives is greater than that of all the other options available to them.

Such a conversion is only a possibility when the church

itself forms itself into a subculture, providing for those within it the social confirmation now lacking in the culture as a whole. Those who are loneliest in the society—i.e., those who have no other group to provide a plausibility structure—are the most likely to respond to a summons to conversion, and the new converts are most likely to persist in their new commitment if they are separated from the larger society by dress and speech, and have contacts only with members of the church fellowship.[32]

The more the choice of doctrine elected by the convert differs from other views in the society, the more painful the conversion will be and the more likely it will be to persist, once the step is taken. The conversion is strengthened when the new convert is enlisted in proclaiming the message to others.

Two comments are in order upon these observations arising from sociological studies of religious faith. The first is that we United Methodists can see much of our history in this description, for we started as an evangelistic society within a church. As a movement, Methodism appealed to large numbers of those who were outside the predominant social groups that provided a plausibility structure. And it cultivated intense groups wherein the experience of forgiveness and sanctification could take root and receive confirmation from others equally serious about their faith.

Subsequent generations of our forebears could appeal to a cultural consensus. United Methodism *was* "mainline" America. But now, when there is no longer a given view of things, when, in its stead, there is a host of choices, then United Methodism can no longer appeal convincingly to a social consensus. We can expect in its place significant diversity and pluralism.

The second comment concerns the individual experience and subjectivity accompanying the necessity for moderns to make choices. If subjectivity is obvious in modern efforts for self-fulfillment, success, and pleasure, it is no less apparent in many testimonies offered for the "electronic church." Reports from those "born again" often center upon an individual experience that leads to individual happiness, success, or other good fortune. God is often regarded as one's individual advocate and ally in the race to make money or to win football games or beauty contests. Viewed in this light, such converts have much more in common with their "worldly" brothers and sisters than might at first be apparent. Both have reduced the basic purpose of life to their personal success and pleasure. This subjective stance, we maintain, is a response to modernization.

2. *Secularization.* Another perspective from which to examine what is occurring in the environment of belief is summarized by the comprehensive term *secularization.* The phenomenon of secularization has been so prominent in the theological discussions of the last generation that we do not need to give extensive attention to it here. Our interest at this point is the experience of secularization as an aspect of the contemporary mood, the pervasive environment that influences Christian belief.

An era of secularization gives its attention to *this* world, rather than to another order that is thought to exist above this one. It looks for natural and visible causes as the explanation for happenings in the world, rather than causes of a more remote sort. Transcendent realities such as God come to be regarded as shadowy, removed, abstract, and, to some extent, unreal.[33] The secular viewpoint sees the world as a set of contingent happenings—i.e., as discrete, concrete events to be studied and understood in their particularity—rather than as manifestations of a larger, coherent purpose.[34]

The perspective influenced by secularization accents the *relativity* of all things. Events and phenomena are to be understood in their relationship to other occurrences and movements, and it is in their relatedness that their meaning is to be discovered. Even doctrines and ideas are viewed in relationship to their historical context. It is not difficult to demonstrate the wisdom of such historical interpretation, yet the problem remains: How, if everything is to be interpreted in relationship to other circumstances, is there to be any point commanding absolute allegiance and loyalty?

The mood of secularization is intently focused on *time* and *change*.[35] It is difficult to speak in terms of God's eternal essence and unchangingness when all of one's life is perceived in the context of time, change, and evolution. An epoch that is concerned about time and change will naturally find more meaning in speaking of the purpose manifest in time and change, the direction in which events are heading, than in speaking of fixed, static realities. Instead of commending the pattern of an eternal order human beings are supposed to replicate in their living and in their ritual, the mood of secularization tends to focus on the role of humans as decision-makers, as choosers, as those who, through participation in history, shape both their history and themselves.

This mood of secularization, we contend, is a pervasive element in our experience in these closing years of the twentieth century, even if the imponderables of life render our human declarations of autonomy and freedom rather hollow at times. A part of the anomaly of our times is that at the very time that there is a renewed sense of our responsibility for the world, there is an accompanying sense that our human powers are incapable of creating the new world we so desperately yearn for.

3. *Shifts in Paradigms.* The ambivalence large numbers of persons feel about responsibility for the world and the inability to change the world can in part be understood as one aspect of a fundamental transformation of perspectives, a "paradigm shift," through which we are passing. By "paradigm," we mean the set of interconnected assumptions

that influence how we interpret the world, the basic model we use to interpret our world. In a time of turbulent, epochal change, few of the confident assumptions of previous eras will any longer command support. We view our world differently. We comprehend it through different models and metaphors.

Surely one of the reasons for the widespread influence of Thomas Kuhn's *The Structures of Scientific Revolutions*,[36] first published in 1962 and revised in 1970, was the detailed analysis he provided of previous fundamental shifts in science. He held that scientific interpretations proceed, not evenly, but by revolutions, transformations, or conversions of the basic paradigms by which the scientists themselves heed and interpret the data at hand. Something akin to these scientific revolutions can be seen in the social sciences. Futurist Willis W. Harman used Kuhn's concept of the paradigm-shift to characterize the cluster of transformations that are necessary if humankind is to have a desirable future on this earth.[37] It is not possible, holds Harman, to solve the problems now before the human race within the terms of the present paradigm—the industrial-state paradigm—for it is the very constellation of values promulgated by the industrial-state paradigm (unlimited growth, consumption, efficiency, etc.) that has brought us to our present crisis.[38]

For our present purposes, it is not essential that we agree on the nature of the emerging paradigm. In conceptual terms, it will probably emphasize the unity and inter-relationship of life, rather than the individualism that has prevailed in Western culture since the Renaissance.[39] In political, social, and economic terms, it is apparent that the emerging paradigm will need to reckon with the flow of power from the industrial nations to the nations that supply raw materials, from growth and consumption to conservation, from expanding the supplies of goods to making do with less, from continuing concentration and expansion of goods and wealth to some equitable means of distributing wealth.[40]

But the nature of the new paradigm is less important than the recognition that we are indeed passing from one paradigm and entering another one. It is now fashionable to term this the post-industrial, the post-modern, or even the post-civilized era. The very use of such terms conveys the intuition of basic shifts sensed by significant commentators of our time.[41]

Certain events provide clues to epochal change in history. In studies of major changes in Western civilization (such as the passing of the Roman Empire, the Protestant Reformation, the Industrial Revolution, the Communist Revolution in Russia, etc.) historians have identified certain rather constant advance indicators of change, indicators that are to be found some time ahead of the societal changes themselves. Among these indicators are:

> Alienation, purposelessness, lowered sense of community.
> Increased rate of mental disorders, violent crime, social disruptions, use of police to control behavior.
> Increased public acceptance of hedonistic behavior (particularly sexual), of symbols of degradation, of lax public morality.
> Heightened interest in, and increase in the amount of, noninstitutionalized religious activities (e.g., cults, revivals, secret practices).
> Signs of anxiety about the future, economic inflation (in some cases).[42]

The symptoms are familiar enough to anyone alive today to suggest some substance to the widespread perception of fundamental shifts in our perceptions of the world.

With these basic shifts in view, it stands to reason that a transformation in the way in which we interpret our world will inevitably be accompanied by shifts in our basic theological views. Herbert Richardson has used the term "public atheism" to describe widespread unbelief and dislocations of belief that occur whenever there is a basic rupture marking the end of one epoch and the beginning of another.[43] Contrary to the assumption of many, the advent of public atheism (or the challenge to belief that is a part of our experience) is not necessarily a foretaste of the inevitable decline of theology. Public atheism, after all, is not an exclusively modern occurrence. Public atheism has frequently been followed, not by an absence of religion, but by its reformulation into a consensus more appropriate to people's real-life experience. Therefore, "modern atheism is not the culmination, or perfection, of the modern world, but a sign that the modern period of history is coming to an end."[44] If we understand the pervasive public atheism or practical atheism as a prelude to a more adequate formulation of Christian faith, we should not be dismayed by doctrinal or theological controversy, but should rather be resolved to see it through to a more adequate witness to the faith within us.[45]

4. *The Force of Contradictory Patterns of Life.* We should not leave this consideration of the difficulty of theological belief today without noting the inevitable connection between our pattern of living and our belief. We have already referred to the way the writer of Psalm 53 immediately saw the connection between sensing the absence of God ("God is not here"), and leading a corrupt, iniquitous life. This understanding, however, is not confined to the Psalms. Jeremiah speaks of a "heart to know" (24:7) and makes the connection explicit between faithfulness in life and knowledge of God:

> He judged the cause of the poor
>    and needy;
>    then it was well.
> Is this not to know me?
>    says the Lord. (22:16)

Or again:

> 'For my people are foolish
>     they know me not;
> they are stupid children,
>     they have no understanding.
> They are skilled in doing evil,
>     but how to do good they know not.' (4:22)

In the New Testament, John's Gospel quotes Jesus as speaking of the one who "does the truth" (3:21). And Jesus says: "My teaching is not mine, but his who sent me; if any man's will is to do his will, he shall know whether the teaching is from God or whether I am speaking on my own authority" (7:16-17).

Knowledge of God, in the biblical writings, is indissolubly linked with a pattern of life. In acting as if the God of justice were not there (the definition of "the fool" in Psalm 53) one is declaring unbelief. In deeds of justice, one is acting out the sovereignty of God in one's being. Knowing and doing are therefore one.

Recent writings in liberation theology have been pointed in their criticism of that form of atheism that denies God by denying or oppressing the neighbor. The struggle of faith for persons who have tasted the bitter effects of racism and the suffocation of poverty is not primarily an intellectual endeavor. It is, rather, how to believe in God when one lives with greed and hatred directed toward oneself, one's children, one's nation, or one's race. The real atheism, says Argentinian Methodist Jose Miguez Bonino, is the denial of "God . . . in the neighbor and the neighbor in God."[46] The person or community struggling to survive against overwhelming odds knows the question of faith and belief to be an eminently practical and urgent one. It is difficult in such a situation to think of God in purely intellectual terms.

We have contended in this chapter that the most formidable barrier to belief is not the cluster of arguments against belief in God, important as they are, but the pervasive unbelief of our times. The frontal assaults on theological belief challenge Christian faith less today than does the unexamined assumption that belief would make no difference anyway. Says Jean-Paul Sartre: "Existentialism isn't so atheistic that it wears itself out showing that God doesn't exist. Rather, it declares that even if God did exist, that would change nothing."[47]

Theological concepts, as we shall later contend, are not merely abstract descriptions of a state of affairs. They arise out of, and are rooted in, certain life patterns. We learn the meaning of theological words by mastering the conduct attending the use of the word. "To lose the meaning of the religious words is not like losing their definitions—it is more like losing the practice with which they were associated."[48] Perceiving the realities of faith is not akin to reading numbers from a computer's display screen. The realities of faith make demands on us. They require a certain justice in our individual and societal relationships. They infringe upon our disposal of our lives. To whatever degree we are unwilling to entertain such an intrusion in our lives, to whatever extent we insist upon living our lives as self-created, autonomous beings, to that extent we are not likely to find it credible that we receive our lives as a gift from the One upon whom we are absolutely dependent.

Joseph Campbell provides an analogy to our present situation in his description of the religious situation of the Native American tribes on the plains in the 1870s and 1880s. The railroad tracks had been laid, and white hunters killed off great herds of buffalo, both to make way for the trains and to deny the Native Americans a livelihood off the reservations. The indigenous religion of the Native Americans had the buffalo as its central symbol. When that symbol was taken from them, their religion disintegrated. The peyote and mescal cults from Mexico became popular. Native Americans gathered to take the drugs, and they experienced visions within as meager compensation for the framework of meaning that had once supported their life and the life of their community.[49]

In a time of rapid and epochal transition, many of the fixtures of our former life no longer exist. In such a time, many persons will return, in a variety of ways, to interior experiences, abandoning the effort of relating their faith to the world outside. Others, facing the same changed situation, will simply repeat the affirmations that grew out of the experience of their forebears and will demand a similar allegiance of others within the church. In this stage of the theological tradition, belief is held by some, not so much because it illuminates life, but because they feel it their duty to defend it. It becomes a matter of "holding religious views rather than being held by them."[50] In such situations, the beliefs themselves have little power to guide life in the world or to attract the loyalty of those not already sharing them.

## C. The Challenge Ahead

In this chapter we have sought to describe the challenges to theology that help place theological issues faced by United Methodists in a wider context. One conclusion that might be drawn from this discussion is that the days of religious belief are numbered and that unbelief is the wave of the future. But that would be a very serious error—and, we might add, a prevalent one!

In the midst of monumental changes in the way we look at our world, it is true that some of the symbols we have understood our world by have been subjected to strain and stress. But this is a matter of the form of *belief*, not of one's fundamental religious orientation to life. In spite of the contemporary challenges to belief, we should not suppose that this age has outgrown religion. The religious need to organize life around centers of loyalty and value persists, even when we lack the symbols to represent those centers. If our gods are those centers of devotion we rely on and trust, then the contemporary world is filled with secular deities. We cannot dispense with religion even if we lack the precise words to give it voice.

Indeed, if religion is the assembly of symbols through which human beings come to terms with the context of their lives, with the otherwise unresolved conflicts of their beings, then religion itself cannot decline until people's lives cease to be problematic.

> The difference between the committed and the indifferent, those with vision and those without it, exists today as it always has, but it seems unlikely that the proportions of the two groups have changed appreciably. If anything, the twentieth century has probably produced more than its share of the committed and the visionary.[51]

The problem for the Hebrews, and perhaps for us as well, was not in having a deity, but in having *too many!* A secular era still has its gods. Many have pointed out, for example, that science functions as a religion for many persons today. In fact, it bears a striking resemblance, in some ways, to some of the ancient salvation myths early Christianity struggled with, particularly the Gnostic myth. In gnosticism, evil is understood as ignorance. We are urged to have confidence in the wisdom to be found through science, wisdom that will redeem us from the forces of ignorance that threaten us.

The plans for salvation through the social sciences have an implicitly religious quality about them. Robert Coles, Harvard psychologist, has referred to forms of salvation through social sciences as "crypto-churches." Even in the face of the atheistic stance of Marxism, it is instructive to note the religious themes that are recapitulated in its ideas about the direction history is taking. The basic Marxist outline of history involves an expulsion from paradise (primitive communism), encountering sinful powers (feudalism and capitalism), birth in humble circumstances (the proletariat), and the expectation of a second coming (the state of communism).[52] This secular salvation story duplicates the Christian salvation story at many important points.

These illustrations are provided to suggest that, even at the formal level, religious themes persist, even in the most secular forms. The principal challenge before theology today is not in developing an area of experience to which theological terms can apply. If we are to develop meaningful "speech about God" we need to find ways to link more closely our experience of God in contemporary life with the historic testimony about God's doings in the past. Without critical engagement, both with historic faith and contemporary experience, we will be tempted to make gods out of our nations, our businesses, our pleasures, or other aspects of creation. These gods are idolatrous. They cannot satisfy. Worse than that, they divide communities and the human family upon this fragile planetary home, investing each of the contending forces with righteous passion to subdue all other contenders.

The reality of our earth is that we flourish or perish together. As Christians, we understand this to be not only a pragmatic observation of a real state of affairs, but the result of our oneness in our Creator, Redeemer, and Sustainer. To invest our life loyalty in these lesser gods is to participate, not in the redemption of the earth and its people, but in its destruction. The real challenge before theology today is to take part in that critical engagement between historic faith and contemporary life that will chasten us when we equate our interests with God's, and that will illuminate the points in our history where God's purposes are to be found.

The challenge assumed in this discussion, therefore, is to find ways of thinking and functioning theologically in relationship to the totality of our lives and ways of correcting our narrow loyalties with the inclusiveness of Almighty God.

# CHAPTER 3

# Functions of Theology in Christian Life

Our interest in this chapter will be to describe theology as it functions in Christian life. The critical need for The United Methodist Church, as well as other branches of the church of Jesus Christ, is to develop skills in reflecting theologically so that Christians will have a firmer grasp on their *identity* in biblical and theological perspective, a clearer cue on the practical *guidance* such an identity implies, and a more winning *witness* to others.

Persons in the United Methodist tradition have consistently maintained an interest in theology's practical bearing on life. This has reflected, not a scorn for the theoretical adequacy of theology, but an overriding concern for the transformation of the lives of individuals and communities.

Modern atheism, as we have seen, has contended that theology is not only a purely human projection, but that, for a variety of reasons, it is injurious and detrimental in its effects on persons today. Christians can hardly deny, of course, that theology is a human work; the words, concepts, and arguments our understanding of God is phrased by are obviously human. Yet that leaves unresolved the primary question: Do these human thoughts, words, and concepts refer to the "way things are" ultimately, to God; or are they artful inventions grounded only in our human wishes, illusions, or projections?

We should insist at the outset that those who attempt to trace Christian theology to mere wish-fulfillment have in no way dispensed with the question of its truth. To point out the origins of astronomy in astrology or the beginnings of chemistry in alchemy does not settle the question of the usefulness or validity of those present-day scientific disciplines. That validity is determined by their adequacy in making a body of experience intelligible. Similarly, Christian theology is most suitably evaluated according to its capacity to interpret the experience of Christian life.

We should acknowledge and immediately disown unworthy uses to which theological phrases are sometimes put. It is possible to take the Lord's name in vain, for example, through trivializing language about God. We are familiar enough with speechmaking in which the name of God is introduced merely to ornament ideas that have no reference—or perhaps are an outright affront—to God. God-language can be pressed into service to win acceptance for programs arrived at on quite independent grounds. The use of theology to cloud issues or to avoid debate on points that really matter is, of course, unworthy and reprehensible.[1] It is a violation of sound theology. In this chapter, we want to describe how theology functions when it is employed in an appropriate way.

## A. Theology in Correlation with Decision, Risk, Mission

1. *God Known Through Event.* The predominant mind-set of modern women and men is functional. By that we mean that our contemporaries wish to know, not the inner essence of things, but how they affect other things and us; that is, how they function. A predictable question from someone seeing a piece of equipment is "How does it work?" or "What does it do?" Or we ask a new acquaintance "What is your work?" or "What are your favorite activities?" We concentrate on verbs at the expense of

nouns.[2] In this trait we bear some resemblance to people of
the Bible, for they were, in some ways, functionalists. They
spoke of God as a force acting in their midst, a concrete
presence to be reckoned with in their daily affairs. They
were not greatly interested in speculative discourses on
God's nature in its innermost essence. They were struck by
God's impact on their lives, which required them to make
critical decisions, to undertake risks, and to consider new
hopes and possibilities for their lives and the destiny of
their nation. Their disputes were not about abstract
questions of the existence of God, but about the character
of the Ultimate Reality that encircled them and what this
Holy One of Israel required of them.

They knew God in connection with concrete events,
rather than in an external order removed from time. They
associated the name of the Deity with events in which their
identity, destiny, and consequent call were disclosed. So
when the Hebrews were seemingly at the end of their
possibilities, with a sea on one side and a pursuing army on
the other, they found that, in spite of all probabilities, they
were delivered. And this event illuminated for them the
providential care they could expect to discern in all events.
What was important to them was that the Mighty One was
not indifferent to the suffering and oppression of a band
of Hebrews in Pharaoh's land. So the name of God itself
took on meaning when applied to this event. They were
explicit about naming God by events. They spoke of the
God who delivered their mothers and fathers at the Red
Sea, the God of Abraham and Isaac, Sarah and Rachel. In
the New Testament, Mary sang in praise of the One who
had "scattered the proud in the imagination of their
hearts, . . . put down the mighty from their thrones, and
exalted those of low degree" (Luke 1:51-52). Early
Christians looking back on the Resurrection spoke of God
as the One who raised Christ Jesus from the dead. The

name of God came to have meaning by the events that were identified as divine acts.

Their theology therefore took shape around recitals of significant events. Probably the earliest and most widely used confession of faith of the Hebrew people was their identification of Jahweh as the One "who brought Israel out of Egypt."[3] They had no speculative treatises upon God's innermost essence. Their creeds were accounts of what had happened in their personal and communal lives (see Deut. 26:5-9).

2. *Self-identity Disclosed Through Event.* Since the theology of the early biblical witnesses was one with the narrative of what had transpired in their lives, it was charged with personal and communal meaning. Theological questions were never detached or dispassionate considerations. They referred to moments of critical importance, when the choice of fidelity or disobedience was glaringly real, when Israel came to know who God was, what God required, and consequently who they, as the people of Israel, really were. It was in their role as actors, as decision-makers, that they struggled with questions of God and of self-identity. Their being was shaped by God's call to them to enter covenant partnership.[4] They knew who they were through participating faithfully in critical events.

3. *Language about God Comprehended as Pattern for Action.* The biblical authors treat faith in God as a stance of one's *whole* life, and not merely the function of mind or spirit. What is disclosed is not so much a set of teachings, as a series of events through which they entered into a new relationship with God.[5] Consequently, their notion of the human being was not defined solely in terms of mind. They characteristically thought of human beings in terms of will. To be a man or woman, for them, meant to strive for something, to aspire, or to will.[6]

God was not considered simply a fact to be discovered

the way we discover common facts in the world. Knowing God was a function of one's entire life. Just as the student of piano, who has become captivated with the possibilities of the instrument and has devoted countless hours of practice and study to performance, will hear more at the concert of a virtuoso pianist than one who has never attempted to play, so the person who has committed his or her whole person to the purposes of God will be the better prepared to comprehend the significance of God's deeds in history. The pure in heart shall see God. Language about God not only refers to what is beyond us, but also refers to a fundamental disposition on our part to relate to the world and our fellow human beings in a certain way. It is the supposition—better, the conviction—that the world under God is a realm of meaning, an arena in which a sovereign purpose is working, a connection of events that aim for a worthy end, even when the meaning and purpose in some events are not immediately apparent. To use meaningful language about God involves having this kind of orientation toward the world and acting on the basis of that orientation. To believe a proposition about God is to be predisposed to act on the basis that the proposition is true.[7] "What we can know depends . . . , to an important extent, upon what we choose to be and to do."[8]

Since saving knowledge of God is a guide to the deep places of life and destiny, a context in which the more profound realities of life can be discovered, then it has little meaning apart from a prior willingness on our part to walk in the illuminated way and to find, in our own experience, the significance theological terms refer to. The appropriate use of theological language is not as a fantasy or projection allowing us to escape the bitter realities of life. Rather, it designates a pattern of life in which the final realities of life can be encountered, a context in which the saving and healing power of God encounters us. Just as we learn the meaning of a word by observing the ways it is used in conversation, so the meaning of language about God takes on meaning when we see, in the context of living, dying, struggling, rejoicing, sinning, and repenting, how speech about God is used. It acquires its meaning by the life experiences it illuminates.[9]

4. *Knowing and Doing the Truth.* In seeking to describe appropriate functions of theology, we are treating fundamental affirmation of Christian theology as indicative of basic orientations to life. If this is the case, then we can make no final separation between affirmations of religious faith itself and the act of utilizing them as one's own perspective, orientation, or disposition before life.[10] Adopting the Gospel as our fundamental point of reference is at once knowing *and* doing the truth. It is in aligning our will with the fundamental orientation of the Gospel that we will be able to discern who Jesus really is, and whether his teaching discloses the way things really are (John 7:17).

Christians who have witnessed to their faith in the midst of deep personal cost and suffering have been in a position to know, more keenly than most of us, how belief and obedience are connected. Dietrich Bonhoeffer, whose martyrdom in opposition to Hitler is well known, has stated it as sensitively as anyone, in his commentary on the calling of Levi by Christ. A set of abstract doctrines about God and the nature of Christ, says Bonhoeffer, makes discipleship unnecessary. We entertain them as formal knowledge. The challenge of discipleship and of belief comes rather in a call of a tangible nature; it is the call to "go with Jesus."

> The road to faith passes through obedience to the call of Jesus. Unless a definite step is demanded, the call vanishes into thin air, and if men [and women] imagine that they can follow Jesus without taking this step, they are deluding themselves like fanatics. . . .[11]

Thus, concludes Bonhoeffer, "only he who believes is obedient, and only he who is obedient believes."[12] He is quick to add that this is not a new kind of work that, of itself, justifies one. It is an external work, as he puts it, but it makes faith possible.

> No one should be surprised at the difficulty of faith, if there is some part of his life where he is consciously resisting or disobeying the commandment of Jesus. . . . Do not say you have not got faith. You will not have it so long as you persist in disobedience and refuse to take the first step.[13]

Thus, when Peter steps out of the boat at the command of Christ, his first step out upon the deeps is an act of faith in the word of Christ. Obedience, then, does not follow believing as a minor premise follows a major premise. The two are interrelated in a single act that is both believing *and* obeying. As it is put in Latin American liberation theology:

> Obedience is not a *consequence* of our knowledge of God, just as it is not a pre-condition for it: obedience is included in our knowledge of God. Or to put it more bluntly: obedience *is* our knowedge of God. . . . We do not know God in the abstract and then deduce from his essence some consequences. We know God in the synthetic act of responding to his demands.[14]

However abstracted from life theology sometimes becomes, at its root it is the report back on what has been discovered by persons who have said "yes" to Jesus Christ. The report takes the form, not of theoretical propositions, but of stories, parables, and powerful images that help convey what was discovered and illuminate those contexts in which we who follow are to find and be found by God. Formal theology is a secondary step derived from the primary report. It seeks to examine critically and reflectively the claims made by these witnesses, to see how the disclosed truths relate to what we know through other approaches, including science, drama, history, and the rest. Doctrines have their importance not only as a cogent presentation of truths implied by Christian experience, but also as designations of the realities encountered in the path of discipleship.

For example, the first word of the disciples in response to the risen Christ was not a theory about what had happened, but rather the witness that the one upon whom they had staked all, and who was executed, was again marvelously alive. His presence and power were with them in a new way. To be sure, they went on to seek ways of saying what they had experienced. The message they bore overburdened the language they sought to express it with. It is clear that they wanted to confess that Jesus was alive, but they also attempted to say that it was a new kind of life. Masterful theologian though he was, St. Paul was driven to use analogies and metaphors (see I Cor. 15:35 ff.). And in the end, it is clear that he is anxious for the Christians in Corinth to believe in Christ's resurrection, not merely because it was true, but because it was a truth that fortified him and them in the ministry they had undertaken together. Outside this truth, the commitment they had made was condemned to futility (I Cor. 15:13-19). But in the light of the resurrection they not only might commit themselves to Christ, but could stand firm in the conviction that their life in discipleship to Christ was not in vain (I Cor. 15:58).

## B. Theology as Practical Guide in Way of Faithfulness

Our basic contention in this discussion is that Christian doctrines, far from being illusions that are inimical to the dignity and maturity of men and women, function instead as practical guides into those contexts where the truth of Christian faith can be discovered and verified. In this section, we will spell out in more detail the way theology serves as a practical guide in faithfulness.

1. *Doctrines that Issue in Action.* If God were only an eternal truth we needed more information about, then the most appropriate stance that we should take in relationship to God would be contemplation and the formation of theory by which we could refer to God's reality. But United Methodists have joined with other major segments of the Christian family in understanding God in terms of God's love for us, and initiative on our behalf, seeking to bind and heal our brokenness. To encounter this reality at all is to acknowledge a claim on one's life. Language about God, therefore, is not neutral, dispassionate language. It is language referring to the stance we are to take toward the Ultimate Reality who has been revealed as our Redeemer. The point of theology is not merely that we should have more information, but that, by the grace of God, we should be more worthy and more faithful. In biblical terms, believing was not an introduction to special knowledge, but an entrance into the *Way,* an appropriate orientation of life that was made possible by the faithful covenant partner God was revealed to be.[15]

Christian doctrine functions in a primary way to orient the believer in the direction in which the realities of Christian faith are to be discovered. "All authentically Christian thinking not only issues in action but is for the sake of action." Furthermore:

> No doctrine has right of place within our Christian theology unless we can show that the denial of it would disturb or distort the pattern of our Christian sharing in that *koinonia* or *agape* which goes back to Pentecost and which I have described as a triangular system of relationships between the triune God, ourselves and our fellows.[16]

2. *Theological Doctrines Aim at Practical Guidance.* It is instructive to think of theological doctrines as a chart, map, or model. In the physical sciences, a model is used to understand a set of happenings and to see how to predict

future happenings. A map represents a kind of model, representing the terrain in a practical fashion so we can get where we want to go. In order to be effective, the map does not need to be a reproduction of the reality it represents. Indeed, it cannot be. It serves its purpose when it provides a practical guide in the journey.

Much less can doctrines pretend to represent precisely who God is. It would be the height of idolatry were we to pretend that we could develop a concept that represented God exactly. God is not One who is scrutinized and compared in the way we examine features of our immediate surroundings. But in the Scripture and tradition of the church, critically compared and examined by reason and our own experience of God, there are certain doctrines that help chart those contexts in which we are brought face to face with God and led in faithfulness to God's commands. These maps do not provide a description of God in God's innermost essence. They do provide fundamental guidance for living in the Way. They point the direction we ought to walk in.

Theologians from a variety of perspectives use different metaphors to describe this practical functioning of theological language. One metaphor is theology as the "grammar of faith," the collection of rules employed by faith in living the faithful life. All people who use a language employ grammar, though only specialists minutely analyze its rules. The purposes of grammatical rules are not served, however, when they are treated as ends in themselves. They are never more faithful to their purpose than when they are employed—probably not even consciously—in articulate self-expression.[17] They find their way into the phrasing of our common speech. Similarly, theology distills rules for the use of language about God, not so we will focus our attention exclusively upon these conceptual ideas, but so we will be enabled to live more faithfully and be more worthy individuals. When the rules are phrased through our lives, they are contributing as they ought to contribute.

The God who is revealed in Christian faith is known as One who is faithful. We are led by accounts in the Bible and by subsequent believers to know those things about God that are necessary for us to live in trust, but we never know enough to satisfy our curiosity about the Divine Being. We never fully know even another human being. What we can know about that person is whether or not that person is reliable and trustworthy. And this knowledge is enough, for it provides a basis for relating to him or her. It is this fundamental guidance for the conduct of one's life that theological perspectives provide. In thus addressing the most profound presuppositions we bring to life, our theology, in large measure, shapes who we are and for what and for whom we will live.

3. *Action Preceding Belief.* Even in the manner in which we have discussed the connection between belief and action, there is a danger in thinking of belief in some fashion as the *theory,* and the conduct of one's life as the *practice* arising out of that theory. In fact, the two are so thoroughly interrelated that it is not possible to make one prior to the other. It is instructive to note that Jesus often confronted people first with a command to join him in the way, and only in the process of walking with him did they come to understand who he was.

For present-day believers, it may well be that they will be moved to engage in faithful acts before they have settled on beliefs about the world that would provide adequate context, or grounding, for those acts. It is as true, to cite only one example, to say that we believe in God because we pray, as it is to say that we pray because we believe. Our acts often "outrun" our belief. And there are areas of Christian belief that will never be disclosed until we are ready to act upon the basis of faith.

To engage in covenant is to pledge ourselves to another

before there is indisputable evidence that the other is worthy of trust. The reason in this instance that action must precede belief is that we discover the covenant-partner is worthy only in the process of trusting him or her and pledging faithfulness to each other. Until the journey is completed, we walk by faith. Faith is pledging ourselves beyond the evidence, and discovering in the course of the journey the worthiness of the one we trust.

In matters of transcendent importance, also, we walk by faith. Believing in God is different from accepting the accuracy of reports concerning the rings around Saturn. Believing in God, more than assenting to a creed, is the direction of a life. Christian doctrines help point the direction in which the realities of life are to be encountered. It is quite likely that we will act our way into new ways of thinking as often as we think ourselves into new ways of acting. In fact, because of its costlier demands upon us, we who have comparative comfort may, like the rich man who came to Jesus, find that it is the act of relinquishment, more than an intellectual problem, that constitutes the most formidable barrier. Theologies now arising out of the context of the dispossessed of the earth center on the practice that must accompany belief. They remind us that the primitive church first set about, not to reduce its understanding of Christ into systematic categories, but to discover new ways of acting in the world.[18] Jesus Christ, says Brazilian Leonardo Boff, presents himself, not as an explanation of reality, but as a demand for the transformation of reality. And it is only in conversion and practical change that we are led by Jesus Christ to God, the Creator.[19]

## C. Theology as Human Response to God's Self-Disclosure

The contention of theology is that although faith "outruns the evidence," it can nonetheless be shown to be an appropriate response to a profound reality, and not just an infantile wish or an immature fantasy about the world. Theological insights, much like our insights on other areas of life, are grounded in illuminating events that are seen to have significance for other events in the past and the future.

1. *Illuminating Events.* Most lives are not lived in time as measured by clocks and calendars. Life lived on clock and calendar time would be even, level, and allocated in minutes, hours, and days of equal duration. Life as it is actually experienced, however, is lived through events with high significance and meaning, interspersed with events of very mundane significance. Calendars have occasions of high celebration with normal working days in between.

Most people, when reflecting on their lives, have no difficulty in recalling a few signal occasions that lend meaning to the rest of their lives. They may recall a wedding, a birth, a death, a career accomplishment, or some serious illness or accident that gives significance to the remainder of their lives. These peak moments, these uniquely illuminating occasions, persist in our memory and help form us into the people we are.[20]

A parallel process is at work in most human relationships. When we think of another person whom we know well, we can probably think of certain occasions that uniquely disclose who that person is. Some action, word, gesture, or expression stands in the memory as a singular occasion marking the character of that person. Some have known people most of their lives, and then have discovered, in some moment of unusual bravery or insight, the capacities that person had all along, thus receiving a new insight into her or his personality and character. Since we never can enter into the personality of other people, no matter how close we are to them, we learn of them through their acts, gestures, speech, and other outward expressions of themselves.

The history of any epoch is written in a similar way. No historian simply writes an even account of everything that happened in a particular period of time. Not only would that be boring; it would be impossible. History is written from a selective perspective. Certain events, particular people, and selected situations are chosen because they are thought to sum up, in singular fashion, the substance of what occurred in a particular era. It is assumed that, in understanding them, one is given an insight into the meaning of their time. Hence, ascensions of kings and queens, wars, treaties, discoveries, elections, social protest movements, industrial developments, and all the rest are the peak moments around which histories are fashioned.

It should not be surprising, therefore, that when people attempt to position themselves in the universe, they select certain happenings out of the chaotic flow of events they pass through by which to understand their origins and destiny. And they select these events in keeping with a fundamental story they believe to be coursing through history. The Bible, as we have seen, is a witness to events that conveyed meaning, purpose, and hope to a people in history. But that description of it is insufficient, for their history was not understood as the working out of an impersonal destiny, but as the disclosure of a Supreme Person with a purpose, who entered into covenant with them and could be counted on to be faithful to that covenant. The flow of events they passed through, therefore, came to be understood as units in an inclusive story that began with the creation of the universe, and would culminate in the final end of all things. Certain peak events led them to understand the nature of the times they lived in and what they could hope for in the future. They "read" their present and their future through the events they had heard about in the past, and this gave them grounds to persist and to hope, even in difficult times. Their historical recollections did not keep them focused upon the past, but were the very source of their confidence for the future. If their forebears had relied upon Jahweh in their need and had not been confounded, then they, too, could trust in the same Holy One and walk unafraid.

Through the recollection and retelling of stories of the past, they formed an overall picture of history and where they fit into it. Otherwise dissociated events then fit together into a universal saga with drama and purpose, giving them hope and strength to stand. They formed pictures of the end of history, sometimes as a natural fulfillment of purposes then active in world affairs, and sometimes as a violent disruption of the present order and the advent of great suffering to be followed by a blessing for those who had been faithful. In the light of the inclusive stories of God's purposes, they could take heart and struggle on in the midst of adversity.

Any story has a focus, and in the story of God's dealing with the people of Israel, the focus, of course, is in the pivotal event all the rest is to be understood by, Jesus Christ. The happenings centering in the life, death, and resurrection of Jesus Christ became for the biblical witnesses the vantage point from which they viewed all else. That which came before was preparation; that which would follow and lead to the culmination of history would, in the last analysis, be confirmation of all they had come to hope for in Jesus Christ. In Oscar Cullmann's phrase, Christ was and is the "mid-point of history," the "final meaning and criterion of all history before and after it, and that in *both* directions. . . . "[21]

In confessing Jesus Christ, Christians of the first century—and every century thereafter—have held that, in this person, we are uniquely addressed by God, that through the person Jesus and the events surrounding him, God disclosed the divine purpose in definitive form, that it is here and not elsewhere that we find the vantage point for understanding the history of which we are a part.

The movement of the biblical authors, therefore, is decidedly from the concrete and particular to the universal. They held, as we have suggested, that this particular event had significance for all possible events to follow, and that the final event would confirm Jesus Christ as Lord. This is the principle of revelation that A. N. Whitehead phrased as follows: "Rational religion appeals to the direct intuition of special occasions, and to the elucidatory power of its concepts for all occasions."[22]

Now that we have noted the focus of faith on certain illuminating events, three comments are in order. First, Christian faith (or even religious belief itself) is not alone in developing inclusive stories to interpret where history is headed. Secular movements likewise develop such interpretations. By their nature, they are religious in form, for they "outrun the evidence" into the future, which no one has seen. They express confidence in the direction of events, expecting the future to provide confirmation of that faith. But presumably secular ideologies also employ implicit structures for interpreting history, even though in doing so they are engaging more in religious, than in scientific, expression. We have already alluded to the secular eschatology found, for example, in Marxism.[23] At least until recently, Western culture has assumed the notion of progress as a guiding principle, presuming that developments as they occurred were essentially beneficial to humankind, and that the human race was proceeding to a time of unprecedented blessing and benefit through the efforts of science and education. Through their ministrations, the essential form of evil—ignorance—was being removed, and rationality and knowledge (usually technical know-how) were replacing this ancient foe. If we have not recognized this overall story, it is probably because it is so

thoroughly appropriated in our culture that it can seldom
be recognized, let alone defended.

A second comment needs to be made. Biblical faith
cannot be understood unless it is recognized that the
biblical witnesses understood themselves to be responding
to God's initiative. They have been recognized by the
Church to have been inspired and unusually sensitive to
the self-disclosure of God, but their witness is, indeed, to a
self-disclosure in which God is the initiator. And the
self-disclosure is that of One who is fulfilling purposes,
who is a faithful covenant partner. In short, the events that
are held to illuminate all other events are those that
disclose a personal being, One who is utterly trustworthy
until time itself shall end. Just as we would not understand
another person if that person did not express himself or
herself in our presence, we would not know God through
these illuminating events if God had not elected to disclose
the divine self through the doings of history.

The third comment is that even as we are confident that
the events themselves are initiated by God, the response to
them is nonetheless human. We are therefore more
confident of the saving power of the events themselves as
they are witnessed to in the biblical record than we are of
the total accuracy of the theories and interpretations that
we, with all our limits, seek to put on them.

We are more assured, for example, that the cross
represents God's saving and liberating act than we are of
any of the many theological interpretations that have been
developed to suggest how that saving effect is wrought.
This is not to dismiss our most disciplined efforts to clarify
the theoretical implications of our faith. It is to recognize
them as human interpretations, which are to be taken
seriously, but are not to be equated with the events
themselves. The United Methodist tradition has espoused
unity on the essential affirmations of faith, and tolerance
for the rest. This is an expression of our confidence in

God's saving power itself, and an appropriate tentativeness about our interpretations of that power.

In "Calendar Tales," Bertolt Brecht has Mr. Keuner say: "I have noticed that we scare away many people from our doctrine because we know an answer to everything. Couldn't we, in the interest of our propaganda, comprise a list of questions which seem to us to be completely unsolved?"[24]

While we are not ready to commend such a list, it is a mark of confidence when a church recognizes the dependability of the basic witness of faith and is willing to allow for future growth in understanding the theories that are presented to interpret such questions.

2. *The Ultimate in the Immediate.* Since theology is a human effort on the part of the Christian community to interpret the interrelationship of historic faith and contemporary experience, it alternates, by its very nature, between facts of immediate experience and affirmations about the Ultimate Reality to whom that experience witnesses. In speaking of God, we are referring to the Last Reality, from whom and before whom all that exists has its being. This ultimate context for our lives cannot be apprehended by us and compared to the statements we make about God to test their validity. To presume that we could manipulate God and somehow capture the Divine Being in human concepts would be the ultimate pretension. To treat the theories and concepts we develop about God as if they *were* God, rather than human efforts to point to God, would likewise be misplaced worship, or, to be more blunt, idolatry.

Persons in the United Methodist heritage have stressed the believer's experience and assurance of God's grace, the witness of God's Spirit in our lives. But even this cardinal emphasis does not equate our experience of God's grace with the theories or categories we use to interpret that experience. What we chiefly need to know about God—

namely, God's faithfulness, God's disposition toward us—can be known with assurance, and generations of Christians testify to that reality. But to have definitive knowledge of God in the true essence of the Divine Being is not given to us to know. That would satisfy our curiosity, but it would probably not equip us to be any more effective in discerning the real issues of obedience and faithfulness to God in our experience.

Lest this seem to claim too little for our theology, let us remind ourselves that even Karl Barth, the late Swiss theologian whose books on theology sag the library shelves, said of theology:

> It can never satisfy the natural aspiration of human thought and utterance for completeness and compactness. It does not exhibit its object but can only indicate it. It is broken thought and utterance to the extent that it can progress only in isolated thoughts and statements direct from different angles to the one object. It can never form a system, comprehending and as it were 'seizing' the object.[25]

Theology does not state how God is in God's own being, but how God is for us.

Keeping in mind that the biblical witnesses encountered God through the medium of concrete events in their history, contemporary Christians must be prepared to be no less "secular" in their understanding of God. That is, Christians today must be prepared to interpret contemporary happenings in the secular world through the light of faith, and the historic faith must be verified through its relationship to contemporary occurrences. It was this Karl Barth had in mind when he said that anyone interested in understanding the book of Romans should engage in reading secular literature, especially the newspapers.

The Scriptures and the historic faith, studied only in themselves, are of little more than historic and antiquarian interest. They burst forth with life when they shed light upon what we can expect of God in our time, where we are to look for God's presence, and what marks it will assume. The stories of covenant and betrayal, of renewal and decay, of incarnation, cross, and resurrection—all these provide powerful illumination on what is occurring in our midst. They disclose the Holy One who is not only our contemporary, but is the very "power of the future" who is luring us ahead in time. It is unlikely that we will comprehend the issues at stake in the worldwide struggle for justice and survival without a grasp of the meaning of the cross. It is similarly unlikely that the full meaning of the cross will dawn on us so long as we remain aloof from those today who, like Jesus, bear the marks of the abandoned of God. Since the reality of God takes on meaning through historical events, in which God discloses who God is, our knowledge of God must take shape as a part of our search for direction and guidance in the course of history. If it were God's purpose merely to illuminate our minds in separation from the external world, then we might expect theology to form itself in a different manner. But since it seems more accurate to say that God intends us to be covenant partners with the Divine, then what is necessary for us is, not a theory to behold, but light for the next step in the "Way."

How, then, do we know when we are faithful in our interpretation and when we are in error? There are four interrelated criteria for theological reflection that we will return to in a later chapter—Scripture, tradition, experience, and reason. All four play an important role in the critical examination of our theology. For the time being, however, we should employ some of the pragmatism that we have noted as a characteristic of theology in the United Methodist tradition. John Wesley sought to spread scriptural holiness throughout the land. While exercising great care to search Scripture and his own experience, he also considered any doctrine from the perspective of its

effect on the central work of presenting God's good news
and winning men and women to discipleship in Jesus
Christ. In a similar way, we hold that Christians are
confirmed in the understanding of faith when that faith
sheds light on the daily round of events, and when it leads
them into further discovery of God's doings in our world.
Were that illumination to fail completely, then there would
be grounds for questioning the faith itself. Put in more
positive terms, we are justified in holding to our theological
convictions when they continue to provide the most
adequate interpretation of our experience, and lead us
into expanding contexts of significance.

3. *Continuing Disclosure in Contemporary Event.* Through
what has been said about the practical nature of God's
self-disclosure, and the way God is known through
"elucidatory" events that illuminate the events we are a
part of, the continuing or progressive nature of our
knowledge of God is apparent. Fervor soon fades if we
have only a noble recollection of God's deeds, unaccom-
panied with any clues about where to find God today. The
"front line" between religious belief and practical atheism,
we maintain, is not so much on the abstract proposition
about God's existence as it is on whether God's existence
does, or would, make a difference. And the difficulty for
many persons who wish to be believers today is that,
despite their intent, what they believe seems to have so little
to do with their world. Talk about God in the context of
such a world seems strangely remote.

Much work is yet to be done in Christian congregations
in clarifying just what we mean by use of language about
God. Many active Christians carry burdensome beliefs that
could be made intelligible with more critical reflection.
The scandal that perplexes many persons is not the central
scandal of the cross itself, but some time-conditioned
aspect of belief that they unnecessarily regard as indispensable. The provisional and conditioned nature of

our theories about God has been acknowledged, yet these human responses to revelation of God are sometimes equated with the revelation of God itself, and thus prove to be more a burden than a source of illuminating God's presence in the contemporary world. Fuller theological and biblical study could free many persons from inadequate interpretations of faith. But another ingredient in the situation must be faced. We cannot finally separate what we know about God from what we are willing to undertake in obedience to God. If it is God's purpose to reconcile us to the Divine Being and to incorporate us into a Covenant people who are joining God's doings in the world, then we can probably expect more light only in proportion to our willingness to live in the light that is already ours. Most of us know enough about God's will to make us uncomfortable with our present level of obedience to it. Additional understanding of God is likely to come when we are hard up against situations of obedience in which we need such light to know what to do.

What follows should in no way reflect negatively on the role of theological scholarship in the church. But it must be said that the moments of greatest clarity for the church have not necessarily come with intellectual breakthroughs in understanding the faith. They have been, rather, when discipleship in the church was such that men and women at critical points in life required light in order to live in obedience to the Gospel. It has been true throughout Christian history, but perhaps articulated only recently in liberation theology, that what we are to believe will be formed in significant measure by our context in life. Many Christians today, including Christians of minority ethnic groups in this country, are finding that God's presence is most real when it is understood in the context of their own struggle for justice and dignity. For them, without romanticizing in the least, there can be no separation between historic faith and their contemporary life. God's reality is clear for them in the midst of their struggle. Because they bring faith-filled and practical questions living out their Christian faith, that faith itself is illuminated, even as it illuminates the next steps in the struggle they are engaged in.

I believe it is the heart of the Gospel that we will find God most directly and vibrantly when we plunge into the life of the world. One of the most frequent responses to Jesus' parables was shock and astonishment. It was the shock of discovering that, in dealing with seemingly routine and near-at-hand questions, they were deciding for or against the promised Kingdom. Both those who had heeded their neighbor and those who had not (for example, in the parable of the Last Judgment) were astounded to know that the ultimate had been present to them in the immediate.

When the theological and the mission work of the Church are related, theology performs a practical task, just as it did in the lives of the biblical authors. We come from experience with urgent questions to raise, questions of direction, hope, survival, and faith. When we search the Scriptures and our own Christian experience in that context, then the Word leaps to life through the work of the Holy Spirit. It becomes God's Word to us in our immediate situation. Though not all questions will be answered, we receive enough light to know the way immediately ahead. Then the work of God's self-disclosure continues in our own life, and the chasm between present experience and historic faith is overcome.

## D. Theology and the Language of Myth and Parable

1. *The Uses of Myth.* There are frequent misunderstandings of the functioning of theology because of the language it uses. It contrasts noticeably with the language of modernity. Often this contrast is focused on the language

of myth and parable that is used in religious discourse, and the gap between this and the seeming precision of scientific discourse. The contrast is sensed by Christians themselves. Indeed, it was the renowned student of the New Testament, Rudolf Bultmann, who persistently contrasted the mythological world-view in which the Bible is cast, to the world-view of contemporary human beings. The whole notion, says Bultmann, of a universe of three stories, the intervention of supernatural powers in earthly events, or the possession of humans by evil spirits, is decidedly incompatible with the notions of cause-and-effect dominant in modern science.[26]

We must admit the somewhat foreign feel of mythological language. But it is pertinent to the present inquiry to note that some element of myth is inevitable whenever we go beyond limited statements about the interconnections of natural events. Langdon Gilkey identifies the elements of myth that quickly accrued to the concept of evolution in the nineteenth century and still may be found. The concept of evolution, useful as it is as an inclusive model for interpreting biological data, is not a precise biological theory. It clearly has been extended beyond the limits warranted for science.[27]

The spread of myths, even in the guise of science, is natural, for every culture must have some myths. Every culture must "locate" itself in some larger order within which its efforts and activities make sense. And in an era dominated by science, it is natural that science itself should manifest elements that point to ultimacy and not merely to discrete measurements and predictions in the natural order. Hence Thomas Kuhn, as we have seen, speaks of changes in scientific perspective that are less like new conclusions coming out of new data than they are like basic conversions or revolutions that cannot be explained strictly on the grounds of evidence at hand.[28]

A mythic element enters whenever we describe the

larger realm of reality our observations fit into, by terms
drawn from our own context. The essence of myth is to
describe the ultimate in terms of the immediate. Eternity is
described in categories drawn from time. Things transcendent are discussed in immanent terms. "Myths give to
the transcendent reality an immanent, this-worldly objectivity. Myths give worldly objectivity to that which is
unworldly."[29] Myths share with parables the characteristic
of a disjunction in language. They are creative and useful
because they force the mind to struggle with the clash
between the two dissimilar realms. Terms meant to refer to
one order are used instead to refer to another, in the case
of myth. Because the only terms we have at our disposal are
terms drawn from our daily experience, references to the
ultimate context we live in, they are likely, in the nature of
the case, to exhibit the fractured characteristics of myths
and parables. This is not attributable to the superstitions or
prescientific nature of their origins, but to the transcendent dimension of their reference.

2. *Myth, Parable, and Theology.* The uses of myth in
theology, therefore, are not to introduce nonscientific
explanations of phenomena that can be explained more
adequately in scientific terms. It is helpful to think of
myths, not as *explanations* of anything, but as *expressions* of
realities that, by their nature, cannot be the object of
scientific investigation; that is, the ultimate context in
which we live.[30]

As expressions of realities, myths evoke a world; they
symbolize a whole.[31] At the same time, they create a
disposition within us toward that world. They confer an
identity upon their users by informing them of the larger
story of which they are a part. One may see readily, for
example, how the Creation narratives of Genesis *express* the
reality of God's creation, as well as the place of human
beings within that world, without representing an *explanation* of the manner in which that world was created.

The Creation accounts form a starting-point for thought, evoking at the outset the attitude that the world is good because it originates from God, and yet, that it is a created good; that is, not to be worshiped in place of its Creator. Humankind's role in the Creation is to be at the pinnacle of the Creation, yet people may not usurp the role of God and claim for themselves what has been declared forbidden. The stories of Creation evoke this attitude toward the whole created order, and that attitude itself forms a stance from which the universe can be explored. Because the Creation is God's handiwork, and not a god, it can be explored and employed for human betterment (including appropriate uses of technology). But because its origin, and the origin of fellow creatures on the face of the earth, is from God, humans may not exploit and despoil the earth without themselves suffering the consequences.

In this process we see the back-and-forth movement described by Paul Ricoeur's phrase: "The symbol gives rise to thought."[32] The symbol (the myth) raises questions for thought. With our inherited myths, we view the world as a given order. But the myths give rise to critical questions about the symbols themselves and the reality they express. Critical, rigorous thinking helps us weed out tendencies to interpret the myth literally and investigate just what its significance is for understanding our world and ourselves. Then we return to the myth with a renewed appropriation, a refined understanding of both the myth and the whole toward which it points.[33]

Just as there is need for calling a world into being through myth, there are also times that prophets and seers need to disrupt a world that has become fated, inflexible. The parable is a metaphor in story form that fractures a world that has become comfortable and stable through myth. It intrinsically violates normal syntax by putting two unlikes side by side. The parables of Jesus provoked astonishment and amazement, since in most of them the

ranking and expectations of normal discourse are re-
versed, and the ones who are said to be first in the
Kingdom are the very persons who, by normal reckoning,
were marginal, irreligious, unpatriotic, and immoral. The
parables were necessary as a means of overthrowing the
smug world of calculation that serious, committed people
had developed, and of proclaiming the kingdom of God as
a new, revolutionary possibility in their midst. Thus the
myth establishes a world; the parable subverts it.[34]

Both the establishment and the subversion of a world are
necessary functions of religious language. We have
already referred to the indispensability of some horizon,
some overall model of the ultimate context of our lives,
both to evoke an attitude toward the world, and to position
us in that world. At the same time, if there is to be creative
change in the world, some alternative model must be
commended, suggesting new possibilities. The parable
depicts an alternative reality, which then commends new
possibilities for those who found no hope or consolation in
the existing order of things. If we are going to be able to
explore constructive new possibilities, we need symbols of
alternative realities, such as those provided by the
parables. It is interesting to note that those engaging in
practical problem-solving find that routinized thinking is a
primary barrier to genuine innovation. One technique for
problem-solving makes use of parable, analogy, and simile
to suggest new ideas and to break out of conventional
solutions.[35]

Myth and parable, along with other forms of narrative,
function for us in directing our attention to mystery
without compromising the mystery through premature
(and misleading) definition. The myth expresses the
reality of mystery without explaining it. It allows for the
contradictions of life, for the complex and unfathomable
realities of love, sin, and reconciliation, without robbing
them of their mystery by explaining them away.

3. *Myth, Parable, and Involvement.* The myths, parables, and other narratives used to communicate religious belief serve to involve us in the reality described. C. H. Dodd's well known definition of parable suggests that the parable teases the hearer into active participation by its comparison.[36] The myth, likewise, does not just convey information. It opens up the reality described, giving us access to what cannot be represented in universal language without distortion and deception.[37]

This emphasis on the capacity of myth and parable to evoke a whole, to promote participation, or to symbolize a mystery, should not be taken to dismiss rigorous categorical thinking and philosophical argument. The symbol, we have remembered, does give rise to *thought.* But with it all, we are remembering that arguments for belief, while important in drawing out the implications of belief, are not, of themselves, sufficient to form and sustain belief. Pascal, speaking of the metaphysical proofs for God, said: "Even if they did help some people, it would only be for the moment during which they watched the demonstration, because an hour later they would be afraid they had made a mistake."[38] The problem with such arguments, important as they are, is that for the believer they are unnecessary, and for the unbeliever they are insufficient.

The myth and parable draw us into them, enabling us to participate in the reality they point to. Howard Thurman tells in his autobiography about the capacity of the story of faith to evoke a response from his slave grandmother.

> When the slave preacher told the Calvary narrative to my grandmother and the other slaves, it had the same effect on them as it would later have on their descendents. But this preacher, when he had finished, would pause, his eyes scrutinizing every face in the congregation, and then he would tell them, "You are not niggers! You are not slaves! You are God's children!"
>
> When my grandmother got to that part of her story, there

would be a slight stiffening in her spine as we sucked in our breath. When she had finished, our spirits were restored.[39]

## E. Theology as Context for Discovery

The function of theology, as we have sought to describe it in this chapter, is described in a way to address the three critical issues acknowledged in the opening chapter of this discussion: identity, guidance, and witness. We have attempted to describe how identity is conveyed on the basis of events and decisions, and how religious belief provides practical guidance. We have stated that theological truth can be commended to others when it renders experience intelligible, when it illuminates our secular experience.

What we have attempted to describe as the function of theology can be summarized in the phrase, "context for discovery." We do not learn Christian theology finally and completely in the way that we master a body of theoretical learning. Learning biblical stories and subsequent Christian thought is necessary, but it is not sufficient. We really learn faith (i.e., find it embodied in life) when we do not so much look *at* the biblical authors and the theologians, but rather when we look *with* them at the everyday realities we experience.[40] The illumination of faith is really employed when it, like a searchlight, is used to discern more thoroughly what is to be found when it is focused on the surrounding scene. We are then aware of faith, but even more, we are aware of the illumination of life that comes when we act in faith's light.

While there is a body of content in Christian faith, the real usefulness of theology is not in remaining focused upon that fixed body of content. Rather, its most useful focus is on the use of basic stories, myths, paradigms, and theories for the assistance they render in discerning the depth of what is happening in our world. The real objective is not copying an object (Christian faith) with the tool of our minds. Our real objective is to adopt the stance of faith so that we can *discover* more fully the depth of the world around us.

This discovery does not take place in the way a camera copies a scene. Discovery is more akin to learning a sport. There is much that we can study and learn about baseball without seeing it played or without playing it ourselves. We can find much vicarious excitement in watching the game played well. But the fullest acquaintance with the game comes in playing it. This involves learning the rules, acquiring the skills of batting, throwing, and running, familiarizing oneself with basic strategies, and other fundamentals of the game. In short, when we learn the sport, we put ourselves in the world created by the game—its rules, pay-offs, penalties—and discover through that context the fullest significance of the game. The experience of baseball is not so much taught, as it is discovered. The horizon of the game is fused with the horizon of our experience.[41]

Christian faith is not a game in the sense of being diversion. It is, however, a context, a basic perspective from which we can discover the deepest significance of the world. It is not a view of another world. It is a perspective on this world, interpreted through the grace of God made known in Jesus Christ. It is a deeper way of seeing, a fuller manner of discerning the significance of the world and our own identity and duty in the midst of that world.

Jean Piaget said that "intelligence is born of action" and that "anything is only understood to the extent that it is reinvented."[42] It would not do grave disservice to Christian faith were we to say that faith is appropriated only as it is reinvented. It springs from action and reflection; it is appropriated as one discovers the realities of Christian life through participation.

Theology, like any other significant knowing, is an offspring of concern and care. It is, to use Albert Outler's felicitous phrase, "agony for *insight*, insight that is supported by further reflection on further experience."[43]

We believe in the act of placing ourselves in the context of certain declarations of the gospel about life, and then, in that context, we reflect about their meaning, illuminating both the belief itself and the realities discovered. This discovery is personal and practical; only secondarily is it theoretical. The stance of Christian faith provides a perspective, a context, from which to begin. As we act in the light of the Gospel, we change both the world and ourselves. It is that large and more intensive meaning of the world and the self that is discovered through action and reflection.

The intimate connection between learning and doing, between knowing and acting, should not be seen as a change in historic Christian understanding. The New Testament word for disciple, *māthētēs*, has its root in the verb meaning *to learn*. The form of learning implied by the root word, *manthanō*, means both to learn by inquiry and to learn by use and practice. To act in response to the Gospel and to learn the meaning of the Gospel are fundamentally two aspects of one response.

"Christianity" is not a New Testament word. It was two hundred years before the Church had systematic statements of the whole of Christian doctrine, and more than one thousand years before the term "theology" was used to signify such comprehensive works.[44] The earliest term they used for their faith was simply "the Way," or "the Road," and those who had faith in Christ were followers of the Way.[45] Expression of faith in Christ entailed joining him on the road. "He who does not take his cross and follow me, is not worthy of me" (Matt. 10:38). The context for discovering the deepest meaning of faith, for them as for us, is "on the road"; that is to say, in the context of the practice implied by the Gospel.

# CHAPTER 4

# Elements in a Living Theology

Even a glance at the life of faith will disclose a variety of elements making up our theological stance. Preeminent among these elements are the images, stories, parables, and other symbols that function in our minds and spirits as representations of Christian faith. Images such as "the Good Shepherd," "Rock of Ages," or the figure of the father welcoming the prodigal son serve as illustrations of such symbols. Our theological stance consists also of clusters of experience, encounters with self, others, the world, or God, which serve to represent the meaning of God and Christian faith to us. For some Christians, the most noteworthy experience will be that occasion, or series of occasions, in which they made a personal decision for Christian discipleship. Others will recall a sublime encounter with beauty, or an instance of healing, and recall such events as part of their theological position.

But actions as well as images and experiences are also elements in any living theology. Out of certain theological convictions, persons feel led to undertake certain actions; e.g., to serve the needs of another, to reconcile two persons who have been alienated from each other, to advocate some just policy or practice. And these actions represent a part of their theology. Some of the actions that provide cues for our theology are liturgical. By that we mean that they are a part of an organized ritual in which persons, by gesture, movement, and word, enact what they believe about God and their fellow human beings. The person who thus kneels or bends the head in praying is, by that movement, saying something about his or her view of God. The person who walks to the altar rail following an evangelistic sermon and kneels, is likewise saying something about his or her understanding of self and of God. Even the building people gather in for corporate worship is itself a statement about what they believe or do not believe about God and the nature of their coming together. Finally, in addition to experiences, images, and actions, our theological stances reflect certain theories about God, self, and the world. We make certain abstract statements we hold to be true; e.g., "God is Creator of all that is," or "Jesus Christ is God present with us." Thus experiences, images, theories, and actions all find a place in a living theology.

We need to add quickly that our theological postures not only involve a variety of elements, but that in our theologies these elements are all interrelated. Certain powerful images and stories guide us in our experience of the world, for example, so that when we come to experience the world, we do so armed with certain predispositions about it. To have learned that "the earth is the Lord's and the fullness thereof" is to entertain a different notion about the world than we would if there were no such image at work in our minds. Similarly, our actions expose us to certain perspectives, which in turn influence how we are going to experience the world. Images and theories influence how we are to experience the world and others. Our experience of the world and of others, in turn, influences what theories or images we are willing to entertain and defend.

Even though it is true that all these elements are interrelated in our experience of living theology, it is possible, for the purposes of this discussion, to suggest

three basic steps that are present in any theology. There is
(1) an experience of the world. This is followed by (2) a
critical reflection upon that experience, interpreting its
significance and criticizing it from the perspective of
certain images and theories. Finally, there is (3) a
reappropriation of the world as it has been experienced
and critically examined.

The discussion up to this point has led us to suggest that
there is a variety of elements present in any theological
stance, and that they proceed in the pattern of (1)
experience of the world, (2) critical reflection upon that
experience, and (3) reappropriation of the world. In order
to convey the notion of interrelationship among these
various elements, we have represented them on a chart as
follows:

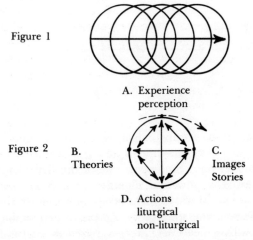

Figure 1

A. Experience
   perception

Figure 2   B.                         C.
            Theories                Images
                                   Stories

D. Actions
   liturgical
   non-liturgical

In Figure 1, we represent the ongoing experience of an
individual as a cycle of experience, critically reflecting, and
acting. Life moves ahead like the arrow moves through the
experiences. In Figure 2, one cycle of experience is
isolated. In this segment there are four interrelated

elements listed. BDC are involved in A. At the same time, ABC are involved in D. In this simple figure, A represents the step of experiencing the world. B and C represent the step of critical reflection upon the world; and D represents a reappropriation of the world through action.

It soon becomes apparent that the four elements illustrated here are in reality the basic qualities of feeling, thinking, and willing that are traditionally used to describe the functioning human being. Figure 1 can be redrawn in keeping with this three-fold description.

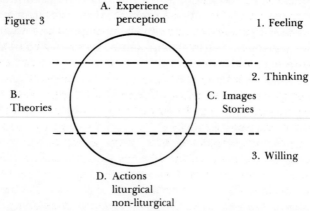

Figure 3

A. Experience
   perception

1. Feeling

2. Thinking

B.
Theories

C. Images
   Stories

3. Willing

D. Actions
   liturgical
   non-liturgical

Examples of human transformation in various movements for social justice may illustrate these elements in operation. For example, the experience of the civil rights movement revealed powerful changes in the lives of people and communities at all three levels. People who had presumably viewed the state of their world as inevitable came to life with a new *experience* or *perception* of their oppression. Mrs. Rosa Parks refused to surrender her seat and go to the back of the bus. The action of a few convinced many others that they could endure an unjust system no longer. It was no longer perceived as inevitable. They therefore began to *act*. The process of acting caused them to *experience* themselves and their communities in new ways. By being identified with the marchers, they now were committed to the movement in the eyes of their allies and their opponents.

This new perception and new action called new *images* and *stories* into being. The biblical story of the exodus and the entry into the promised land, for example, assumed central significance for the civil rights movement. Songs were used to reinforce these stories. Whole new histories were written, stressing the figures of the past who did not give in to the forces of racism. And in the process it was necessary to develop new *theories*. Civil rights leaders taught new theories about the makeup of the community, the nature of social change, and the techniques of nonviolence. They taught the economic facts about the power that actually existed in the black community. In this example, all four elements were interrelated as people went about the work of transforming their lives and life in their communities.

If theology is to bear any relationship to the transformation of life that is a central concern of United Methodist tradition, then it must likewise be related to each aspect of life—feeling, thinking, and willing—and not be confined to any one aspect by itself. Indeed, one of the dilemmas that now confront theology in United Methodism—and perhaps in most of the "mainline" Protestant denominations—is the confinement of theology and religious faith to one of these elements alone. Although the process of living inevitably involves elements of feeling, thinking, and willing, many people's theological orientations are stripped of vitality by becoming isolated in one sphere or another. Some, for example, emphasizing the element of feeling, will exalt a certain form of experience as the norm for all Christian life and theology, and see other aspects of faith and life as instruments toward that end. Others will accent thinking to the exclusion of virtually all else.

Religious and theological integrity for such persons will
consist of finely wrought doctrines or systems of doctrines
to which one should give intellectual assent. Still others will
focus on willing as the definitive description of adequate
theology. They will emphasize one's personal will as the
singular virtue and will stress the manner in which that
will, perhaps joining itself with the perceived will of God,
phrases itself into acts of Christian love. More frequently,
the emphasis on will is heard to suggest that Christian faith
is simply a series of charitable acts toward one's fellow
human beings, and that that sums up the substance of
theology.[1]

A moment's reflection will suggest ways certain prominent theological positions concentrate on one of these
elements at the expense of the others. Certain forms of
revivalism, and what is now termed "charismatic" faith,
clearly exalt one's feelings as determinative for faith and
theology. Certain activists would seem to make the will the
determinative concern for theology. Yet others, of course,
focus on thinking at the expense of the other two.

As we sought to suggest in the last chapter, a living
theology functions in the life of the whole person and the
whole community. The Bible frequently speaks of loving
God with all one's heart, mind, and strength. Even the one
word, "heart," means all one's emotion, reason, and will. It
is a collective term for all one's discerning and acting
powers.[2] If we are to love God with all our heart, soul, and
strength, and if theology is to have a living relationship to
all of life, then it is clear that the elements of feeling,
thinking, and willing will have to be brought together in
their rightful integral relationship.

When we examine how such elements actually work in
our ordinary lives, there is, in fact, a dialectical relationship
among the elements of feeling, thinking, and willing. By
"dialectical" we simply mean that they operate in tension
with one another. This is the action we spoke of at the

beginning of the chapter when we referred to experiencing a world, reflecting critically upon that world, and acting on the basis of the resulting renewed judgment of the world. We shall now examine the manner in which our theological reflection includes all these three elements.

## A. Feeling: Experiencing the World and God

Theology in United Methodist tradition has consistently stressed the importance of experiencing God's presence. Our experience of God is more akin to *perception* of the world than it is to *propositions* about an absent object.[3] When religious faith has been real for persons, they have experienced God, not as a detached element of their awareness, but as a deeper way of interpreting, a more profound way of seeing the events they were a part of. Encounter with the world is simultaneously experienced as a continuing encounter with God.[4] To the biblical authors, the being of God took on meaning through its association with certain critical events they had passed through. Their experience of God was inextricably tied to their political and social history. Their experience of national independence, of economic injustice within, of defeat and exile—all these were understood by their seers not merely as political triumphs or reversals, but as fulfillments of divine promises or as aspects of the divine judgment. Even their suffering and humiliation came to have meaning, not as a repudiation of God's care for them, but as the way God works healing for the many through the suffering of God's servants (Is. 40–55).

In the New Testament, the event many would have thought to be the most definitive repudiation of belief— the cross—came to be regarded as the definitive point at which humans encounter the love of God.

United Methodists in various parts of the country, on being asked to name those occasions in which they

encountered or were encountered by God, frequently
listed common events in their lives or the life of their
community that had acquired special meaning as signs of
God's presence. For many, it was some crucial illness in
which they were both reduced to a sense of impotence and
lifted up by strength they acknowledged was not their own.
Others found themselves addressed by God in the context
of some highly important decision or risk. Others
struggled with the question of God around some serious
reversal in their lives. Virtually none thought of God at the
outset as a set of theories or doctrines (though those
questions arose later) but rather as the deeper meaning of
the events they had passed through.

This is to say that the experience of God typically is the
encounter with events *experienced as* the presence of God.[5]
Not everyone who beheld a bush burning in the desert
turned aside to interpret its more profound meaning. In
other words, to state the obvious, the experience of God is
not as plain and clear as seeing a tree or a stone in front of
us. Happenings experienced as the presence of God by
some, elicit no such interpretation from others.

Lest this seem to make our experience of God a highly
subjective and tenuous matter, we should hasten to add
that our experience of even the most common elements of
experience includes the possibility of alternative interpretations. In all of our experience, we confront a reality that
is outside of us. We also bring with us an interpretive
framework that is not a part of the situation presented to
us. We could never see stones and dogs and bushes if there
were not something "out there," but they *are* what we
perceive them to be only when we bring to the experience
some images, models, or stories by which to interpret
them. In our experience of common objects, we often
become aware of the crucial role played by our interpretive
apparatus. Walking through even familiar territory in the
dark, we struggle with our minds to make sense out of the

shadowy shapes and objects around us. If we are unusually wary, we may think we see the shapes of lurking muggers behind a light pole. A bush beside a country road appears to be a sitting animal. Our mind and imagination struggle to render the chaotic shapes intelligible.

Recent discussions in the philosophy of science have shown that, even when great care is taken to be objective and dispassionate in an enterprise, there is a significant influence exerted by models and *paradigms,* by the passion and intuition the observer brings to the observations. A "paradigm" is a basic model or pattern that is used to interpret the world. The view that the sun is the center of our universe is one paradigm, for example. And these elements of interpretation and passion, far from nullifying knowledge, may well be its indispensable precondition. The questions that are asked and the data deemed relevant to answer the questions are not found in any significance inherent in the data themselves, but rather arise out of basic models of the physical world, pervasive paradigms, that are brought to the investigation. Our inquiry into nature is "theory-laden."[6] Thomas Kuhn and others have demonstrated how change in scientific pursuits takes place, not in a gradual and methodical fashion as new data are gathered, but in discontinuous leaps, revolutions (we might call them conversions) in which gifted innovators by bold new intuitions develop entirely new models for comprehending the world. To those schooled in the old model or paradigm, the innovator is a heretic (if not mad) because she or he is, in effect, living in a different world. But before such bursts of insight occur, investigators struggle for years (if not generations) trying to fit aberrant data into the models and paradigms they have become familiar with.[7]

Michael Polanyi has stressed the personal involvement in any scientific knowing, holding that Copernicus turned his back on the seemingly obvious fact of the sun's rotation around the earth, and embraced instead the model of the earth revolving around the sun, partly out of the intellectual delight of the new theory.[8] The gaps between scientific interpretation of the world, says Polanyi, are logical gaps, which are leaped only by a passion for discovery.[9] And after the investigator has developed a new paradigm, the personal passion that first inspired the leap is now consumed in the desire to convert everyone to the new way of looking at things. He continues to describe the process of scientific innovation:

> Proponents of a new system can convince their audience only by first winning their intellectual sympathy for a doctrine they have not yet grasped. Those who listen sympathetically will discover for themselves what they would otherwise never have understood. Such an acceptance is a heuristic process, a self-modifying act, and to this extent a conversion. It produces disciples forming a school, the members of which are separated for the time being from those outside it. They think differently, speak a different language, live in a different world, and at least one of the two schools is excluded to this extent for the time being (whether rightly or wrongly) from the community of science.[10]

The "conversion" Polanyi speaks of is the change from one paradigm to another. A new paradigm draws the investigator's attention to new data and to new ways of reconciling previously anomalous data into a meaningful new pattern. There are instances in which it is profitable to have two different models for the same phenomenon. The behavior of streams of electrons can sometimes be explained more satisfactorily as particles, and at other times as waves.[11] The choice of models, or the combination made of them, hinges in part on the aspect of the question one is seeking to address.

All this is to suggest that, even in the highly disciplined observations of the sciences, the data are not simply "out there" waiting to be registered on our sensory organs, but are instead governed by the interests and passions the scientist brings to them, the models and images that are in the investigator's mind, and the interests and concerns that that person carries into the investigation. As Albert Einstein put it, "It is the theory which decides what we can observe."[12]

This brief excursion into other forms of experiencing the world is not taken to suggest that our experience of God and the experience of the physicist or chemist are somehow the same. They are not. We do mean to suggest, however, that they are not utterly dissimilar. We do mean to repudiate the notion that scientific observations of the world are absolutely objective, and that they are to be contrasted with the purely subjective observations (or should we say projections?) of the religious believer. In fact, "science is not as objective, nor religion as subjective, as these two opposing schools of thought assume."[13]

Scientific observation and religious belief are to be distinguished, not because one is absolutely objective and the other subjective, but because one (the experience of God) is comprehensive in its reference (holding implications for every time until the end of time, and for every world that is or is to be), whereas scientific observations, when applied aright, pertain only to specific cause-and-effect sequences. Furthermore, religious beliefs are to be distinguished because of their personal implications for the believer. They concern one's whole life and destiny, whereas the outcome of a scientific observation may have only an intellectual interest. A greater investment of one's own images and world-views is involved as the scope of our observation expands, and as its personal relevance to our situation increases (see Figure 4).

It calls for little commitment or involvement, for

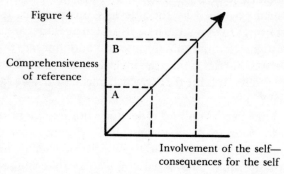

Figure 4

Comprehensiveness
of reference

B

A

Involvement of the self—
consequences for the self

example, to announce that the sum of two and two is four (Figure 4, A). It is of much more significance to hold "The earth is the Lord's . . . . " (Ps. 24:1; Figure 4, B).

Our point so far is that our experience of God is akin to our perception of the world, even if there are important distinctions to be drawn. The person of faith experiences and relates to the world as Creation. The believer approaches events with the expectation that they are related—even if that relationship is obscure or seemingly contradictory—to the purposes of God, the Final Reality who is to be trusted and loved. With St. Paul, we can rest assured that nothing can separate us from the love of God in Christ Jesus our Lord (Rom. 8:35-39).

We can illustrate this perception of the world experienced as the presence of God, in Jesus' own teaching. His characteristic way of teaching was not through finely worked theories. Rather, we are told that he said many things in parables, with Mark even overstating it a bit by suggesting that he taught in *nothing other than* parables (Mark 4:34). The remarkable quality of the parables is Jesus' contention that the things of God are to be found in the most conventional happenings, happenings so credible and natural that they disarmed his most violent critics. The reign of God, he said, is not a completely different world, but is experienced as the deeper meaning of this one. The experience of the Kingdom is intertwined with our experience of the world. The healing grace and mercy of God bursts about us in seemingly commonplace events.

In this section we have sought to describe our experience of God as bearing some important resemblances to our experiences of the world. Without making the two the same, we have held that our experience of God is the "construing" of our experience as the presence of God, even as we construe objects and situations to have specific meanings. When a person becomes a Christian believer, there is a new model by which he or she interprets the world. To experience God's forgiveness and to know new life in Christ is to regard one's past, present, and future in a radically different context (see II Cor. 5:16).

## B. Thinking: Critical Reflection upon the World

If our experience of God is akin to our experience of the world around us and our experience of other persons, it must be added that we do not experience God as one object among all the other objects that are part of our world. This is a real distinction between God and an idol. An idol is one among others; God is in, with, and behind all. The task of theology, therefore, is not so much to isolate a single existing Being and to demonstrate the reality of that One's existence, as it is to call attention to the reality of God as it is known through all our knowing of the world and other selves. God is not one instance of an existing being; God is the basis for there being anything at all.

Believing in God, then, is a perspective we bring to all our observations of the world and of other selves. It is a stance, a perspective we embody in all our thinking, willing, and feeling. As the basic orientation, the primary standpoint from which all other realities are interpreted and known, religious belief does not lend itself to the same

kind of argument and proof that is possible for less
comprehensive statements about reality. Belief in God and
the view of the world that attends it are more comparable
to the basic models and paradigms that inform the
scientific investigations of an era, than to any specific
theories that come out of those paradigms. Those
paradigms are changed; scientists do adopt different
pictures or paradigms of the universe and employ them in
their studies. But basic paradigms change only with leaps
of the imagination that overcome the logical gaps. And
they are surrendered with great reluctance, even when the
observable data do not fit into the dominant paradigm in
use.

Religious belief is comparable to a paradigm in that it is
the overcoming of a logical gap. Religious belief cannot be
shown to be a worthy stance apart from the experience of
adopting it and seeing life from its perspective. It is so
pervasive in its scope that, when one has embraced a basic
religious belief, the world is not so much an evidence for
the belief as it is an illustration of the comprehensive belief
that informs all our perception. In religious language, to
change one's basic orientation toward the world is a
conversion, a transformation of one's whole perspective.
"From now on, therefore, we regard no one from a human
point of view; even though we once regarded Christ from a
human point of view, we regard him thus no longer.
Therefore, if any one is in Christ, he is a new creation . . ."
(II Cor. 5:16-17).

In an era in which there was widespread agreement on
basic models of reality, agreement on religious belief that
accompanied and undergirded that construction of the
world was not difficult to find. In a world marked by
pluralism and diversity, there is no single "sacred canopy"
under which all can gather. We bring significantly
different presuppositions about the world to our observations of it. It is small wonder, therefore, that our

theologies are diverse; and that, for many, the notion of theological language itself is not merely invalid, but meaningless. In the following paragraphs we set forth some of the elements involved in our activity as thinking beings.

1. *Myths, Stories, and Parables.* Stories are not only intelligible in themselves, but they render other elements intelligible. We often say of someone, "If you knew what she had been through, or if you were aware of his background, you would know why the person acted the way she or he did." That means that the story of their former life would provide clues that would make their present actions intelligible.

The story presents us with a whole situation in whose context certain actions are appropriate. We know that when Jesus was accused of irreligious and immoral acts, he responded by telling stories in which such acts were not only permissible but "needful." So there was the same cogency and appropriateness in keeping company with and eating with sinners as there was in a woman's rejoicing when she found a lost coin, or a shepherd's celebrating when he found a sheep that was lost, or a father's throwing a party for the community when a son returned from a distant country (Luke 15). Those situations depicted by the stories provided contexts in which extraordinary acts were not only acceptable but required.

Stories also convey identity. On successive evenings a few years ago, a national television audience saw a single story weave its way through generation after generation, in Alex Haley's reconstruction of his family history, *Roots.* It was a moving experience to see each new generation taken aside by a mother or father and told the story of an African warrior, torn from his native soil in his youth, brought to be a slave, but steadfastly refusing to surrender his real identity by accepting the slaver's name for him. And in the recital of that story, the new generation received a notion of its lineage, a picture of its identity, and a new determination to be free people.

Religious belief involves the recitation and hearing of stories that evoke a picture of the realms of reality. They are not demonstrable theories about reality, but illuminating stories that, by their light, render the events we pass through intelligible. To hold, therefore, as Christians do, that the cross is the center of an inclusive story told throughout the Bible, predisposes a person to understand suffering and hope in a distinctive way. The sheer, brutal irrationality of suffering is not eliminated, but is provided with a context in which suffering, willingly undergone, is the source of help and healing. The story of the cross, the "old, old story," predisposes us to view life from a certain perspective and to find our hope in a particular way. It alerts us to look at certain happenings with a particular stance. A banner portrayed a mushroom cloud with a cross emblazoned on it. The words printed on the banner pleaded: "Please reflect on the sufferings of Christ and how they relate to the bomb today." And this is just the point. The sufferings of Christ provide the pattern, the paradigm by which we see the obscenity of nuclear war, and the preparation for it, in the name of security, for what it is.

The myths and stories of faith provide the believer, not with a replacement for reason, but with a beginning point for the practical reasoning activity. We cannot dispense with these beginning points, any more than the scientific enterprise can abandon having some basic paradigm by which to conduct the larger investigations. Images and stories are employed by the practical needs of living.

The heart must reason; the participating self cannot escape the necessity of looking for pattern and meaning in its life and relations. It cannot make a choice between reason and imagination but only between reasoning on the basis of adequate images and thinking with the aid of evil imaginations.[14]

We think, therefore, with the aid of images. We employ stories, myths, and images when we experience God in, with, and under our experience of the world and other selves.

It should be noted that the function of basic stories may also be to disrupt prevailing arrangements in the name of a new possibility. Stories, myths, and parables convey imagination and, by implication, provide a way of reflecting critically on the way things are in any given society.

Imagination is sometimes identified with fabrication. But it has a deeper meaning. One of its definitions is "the ability to represent the real more fully and truly than it appears to the senses and in its ideal or universal character . . . ."[15]

The prophetic imagination is the capacity to draw upon the stories of faith and to represent the real state of affairs in contrast to an existing state of affairs that presents itself as inevitable and definitive.[16] Just when there were those in Israel who undergirded the ease and prosperity of some, holding that it was the blessing of God, there came prophets who employed the story of the call and the covenant to declare another reality, as yet not appearing to the senses, by which the present unjust order was disrupted and violated. The use of the imagination provided a way of challenging the dominant reality.[17]

The prophet senses the full gravity of the situation by seeing it through the story of God's inclusive purpose and the blessing that is promised for Israel and for the nations through faithfulness to the covenant. So, when the dominant consciousness is proclaiming that all is well, the prophet, drawing upon the stories of faith, declares a controversy that Jahweh has with the people. And when the nation senses that it is spent and forsaken, the prophet declares the words of healing and comfort, assuring those who have suffered deeply that their tragedy is ending (Is. 40–55).

The language of story and myth is used by the prophet to deliver the people from the inevitability in which they seem to be locked. Symbols out of the story of God's dealings with them are offered as ways of imagining an alternative future. The force of this alternative future breaks the power of the old order and its claim on them. "The prophetic imagination knows that the real world is the one that has its beginning and dynamic in the promising speech of God and that this is true even in a world where kings have tried to banish all speech but their own."[18]

The prophet is involved in critical reflection upon contemporary events, using the story of a nation and God's relationship to it as the starting point for thought. The story becomes the paradigm their situation is illuminated and judged by. The most despondent situation is not to be faced with formidable odds—the most forlorn situation is to be facing such odds without any ability to imagine an alternative to the present. The prophets, reflecting on the basis of story, found it within them to imagine another state of affairs determined by the promises of God. And in so doing, they provided an alternative future for the people of Israel.

Critical reflection upon the basis of story employs an alternative between the illuminating story and the events through which the believer is passing. As the believer, struggling for insight and direction, reflects critically on the present predicament, utilizing the biblical witness as his or her basic model for understanding, the true dimensions of the situation come into focus. The seriousness of the sins of the people is seen. The significance of political choices is read, not merely according to the short-term judgment about clever maneuvering and the manipulation of power, but according to the purposes of God disclosed throughout the biblical record. The Bible illuminates the current context. On the other hand, the current situation helps one enter imaginatively into the world of the Bible. The Bible lives as the events that it records are warmed by the heat of our present involvements.

As the story of our basic informing events, the biblical revelation is never mastered with a meaning that can, once mastered, remain static. It assumes refined shape as it is used as the starting point for critical reflection. It is comparable to people living in a valley, who from time to time climb a magnificent mountain that walls one side of the valley. The mountain is a constant point of reference and source of perspective as they go about their affairs in the valley. Its peak is the first to reflect the light at dawn, and its slopes are bathed with the sun as it sets at dusk. Its contours and peak change color and shape to mark the shift of the seasons. Its beauty is the backdrop for all that transpires.

Each time they climb the mountain, they discover that they learn, not merely more about the mountain, but also more about the valley in which they dwell. As the mountain becomes more and more familiar, they notice more of the shape and beauty of the valley terrain. The noise and immediacy of their doings in the valley are hushed, and there is a timelessness that unveils new perspectives for those who return to their life below. Thinking in the light of the stories, myths, and parables of the biblical witnesses involves a similar alternation between historic faith and contemporary happening.

It is because of this changed perspective that it is true to say, as Edward Schillebeeckx does, that the believer not only interprets experiences differently, but to a real extent lives in a different world than the nonbeliever.[19]

2. *Theories.* The person of faith can be confident within that faith only so long as she or he is confident that that faith is not illusory, but rather is reflective of the way things

really are. Faith outreaches the capacity of our minds to demonstrate, but it cannot survive in a mature fashion as a deception or illusion about the real world. Like a basic scientific paradigm, it cannot long survive evidence that totally disproves it.

It belongs to the proper functioning of theology, then, not merely to think on the basis of fundamental stories and images of the faith, but to examine the implications of the experience of the Christian Church, to examine what things are held as true. Whereas the Bible tells the story of God's dealings with humankind and the creation of the world, systematic theology seeks to set forth a coherent account of what is taught about God, about Creation, humankind, sin, redemption, the cross, and other basic elements of the biblical message.

Not only is the message of the Bible expounded in this reasoned way, but the implications of faith are compared to what we may know of ourselves and our world through other disciplines. In this step of theology, we examine various theories about the natural order, about the makeup and functioning of human beings, about history, and all other areas of human learning, and seek to develop a picture of the world that is consistent with these and with faith.

Whether such a theory is developed into a full theory about the universe and ultimate reality or not, the basic assumption informing the enterprise is that reality is one, and we cannot entertain notions about the world and affirm biblical stories that are clearly inconsistent with one another.

Conventionally, critical theoretical reflection has been conducted with the aid of work in philosophy. In recent theology, the work of psychology has been given a more prominent role, with theologians working to relate the insights into human nature and the representations of human beings that are found in biblical revelation.

Christians involved in struggles for liberation from economic, social, cultural, and political oppression have stressed the need to involve economics in the critical reflection we are involved in. Juan Luis Segundo has expressed this conviction systematically in *The Liberation of Theology*.[20] Even before we come to the theological task, says Segundo, we must have a commitment to the poor and to the questions arising out of the specifics of our economic and political situation.

The results of this critical reflection will vary greatly with the stance the Christian brings to it. But it is from this work that creeds and confessions come. *Systematic* theology attempts to state the important implied truths in a comprehensive and coherent fashion. *Apologetic* theology seeks to state the affirmations of Christian theology in a fashion that defends against the attacks of others and commends Christian faith to those who do not now believe. *Dogmatic* theology states the truths in a definitive fashion, and the name implies that there is a legislative authority in some recognized division of the Church lying behind the affirmations. *Biblical* theology seeks to articulate the implicit thought-forms of the biblical witness in an organized fashion.

It is this biblical portion of theology that is more readily recognized, perhaps, as traditional theology. It is significant and crucial. But the exposition that has gone before and that which is to follow suggest that it is not the only, or even the most important, part of the theological labors of the Christian Church.

## C. Willing: Theology and Action

In this chapter we have suggested that elements of theology correspond to the feeling, thinking, and willing activities of our lives, and that theology must be related to all three. One cannot separate thinking and willing from feeling (one's perception of the world and God), nor is a person's feeling and willing conducted without the involvement of thought and reflection through the use of images and more abstract theories. We turn now to the element of willing, which we contend is intrinsic to theology. We are considering willing, or intentional activity, as incorporated in the practical guidance of life, one's pattern of action; as well as the symbolic activity involved in liturgy and ritual. And we are contending here, as we have throughout the discussion, that one's actions are an integral part of one's theological position.

1. *Patterns of Action as Source of Perception.* It is a commonplace experience to discover that we see things differently when, for any of a number of reasons, we are involved in new patterns of action. We have already alluded to the change of perceptions of self and community when persons become visibly involved in some community action. Demonstrations and marches taking place in the 1960s and early 1970s in this country often had, as one of their principal effects, the change of perception that came to those who were physically identified with a cause and were treated by the public and public officials primarily as representatives of that cause. "Nothing radicalizes you like being gassed," reported one student in the late 1960s to his theological professor.[21]

When our behavior changes, our attitudes change to keep pace, and our minds struggle to make this new experience intelligible. The mind modifies existing views in order to accommodate to the new reality encountered in action.[22] One of the salutary results, for example, that sometimes occurs when minority persons and women are promoted to places of authority in business and society, is that persons who hitherto harbored racist and sexist notions about others' alleged inferiority find themselves reporting to these people, who are now their superiors. Though there is no automatic assurance that thinking will change in the direction desired, it often does. Persons find that in acting differently toward others they have to think differently about them as well.

In willing a pattern of life, we are implicitly testifying to a view of the world such actions appropriately fit into. What the world will appear to us to be rests in part on the pattern of life we have elected to follow. Faith is both a decision and a means of perception.

> When a person dares to live on the basis of the unseen, to draw strength and standards not from the visible world, but from the invisible reality of God, to focus on a word of promise (the Gospel of Christ), then he or she achieves a new perception. This provides no new information concerning things, but is, as it were, a new vision of reality as a whole.[23]

We are reasserting here what was stated at the beginning of the chapter: human beings do theology as whole people. In biblical terms, they know God with their whole heart, which includes thinking, feeling, and willing. We should expect, therefore, to find confirmation in experience for the proposition that thinking and acting are reciprocally related, and that both have a practical bearing on what we are capable of feeling or perceiving about God and the world. In the Christian life there are some insights about God that are gained through practice and action before the theoretical grounds for such insights are understood.[24] And, put in other terms, there are persons for whom the language about God is meaningless and nonsense simply because they have willed a pattern of action that is dissonant with the more profound declarations of Christian faith.

Throughout tradition, our knowledge of God has frequently been compared to the profound ties of a man and a woman in marriage. In both relationships, knowledge is preceded by an act of the will: the covenant. Thought and reflection are involved in the covenant, to be

sure, but, in the nature of the case, not all the evidence can
be considered before one enters the covenant. The quality
of the relationship is, in many ways, yet to be formed. And
the formation of the relationship hinges to a large degree
upon what the two parties have decided that it will be. As
they act in the pattern of loyalty to each other, more and
more of the beauty of that loyal relationship is disclosed to
them. What they perceive in each other is disclosed, not as
information available to one who is casually related, but as
the result of lifelong commitment. It should be noted that
this is not projection. Just the opposite; it is a more
profound way of perceiving. In a parallel manner, faith is a
decision for a pattern of life, in whose context the deeper
realities of life are encountered and perceived.

The relationship between what one can perceive about
God and the pattern of life one is prepared to enter is
reflected in the biblical records themselves. But we have
accented the abstract and theoretical so consistently in
Western theology that we have at times been inattentive to
this reality. Liberation theologians, black theologians, and
feminist theologians are reminding us with renewed
sharpness of the inextricable ties between the pattern of
living and our belief. They have used the difficult term
*praxis* to refer to "the critical relationship between theory
and practice whereby each is dialectically influenced by the
other."[25] Among liberation theologians, there is renewed
stress on theology's context in a "historical project" to
which one has committed oneself, and for the sake of
which one's theology is undertaken. Theology in this style
is not solely a library project but is a commitment for the
sake of the poor.

2. *Action Rooting Theological Symbols.* Theological symbols find root in our lives and imagination when we will to
act on the basis of them, even if those symbols are
incompletely understood. If we mean by "belief" the
capacity to rely on a truth in action (and not merely the

assent of our minds to a doctrinal proposition) then there is powerful truth in the dictum: "We must understand in order to believe, but we must believe in order to understand."[26]

At the close of his lucid study of the symbolism of evil, Paul Ricoeur alludes to this statement, which means that, in order to discover the power of any religious symbol, it is necessary to make a "wager" on behalf of the meaning toward which the symbol points. "Never, in fact, does the interpreter get near to what his text says unless he lives in the *aura* of the meaning he is inquiring after."[27] This is not to say that it is out of sheer will that we create the truth of a symbol. Rather, we live in its light and then reflect critically upon it. It is this alternation between willing a pattern of life and reflecting critically upon the meaning discovered in its light that helps theological symbols come to life.

It is in the course of action and commitment that we have a sharpened focus on the meaning of faith. Persons of United Methodist heritage will recall the famous entry for March 4, 1738 in John Wesley's journal:

> Immediately it struck into my mind, "Leave off preaching. How can you preach to others who have not faith yourself?" I asked Peter Bohler whether he thought I should leave it off or not. He answered, "Preach faith *till* you have it; and then, *because* you have it, you *will* preach faith."[28]

The meaning of theological symbols is aided somewhat by clear definitions of what the terms mean. But the symbols themselves come to life when one is introduced into a context in which the symbols find a natural setting. It is in the context of intended practice that symbols such as the terms, "sin," "grace," and "reconciliation" find their richest meaning. Definitions or narratives that they are used in help alert us to presence of the reality when we meet it. It is the lived experience that genuinely introduces what the symbol means. Martin Luther was not one to deprecate the role of learning in the faith, but in his commentary on Psalm 5, he makes it clear that learning is lower in importance than the practical experience of living. He says that one "becomes a theologian by living, or rather by experiencing death, and condemnation, not by mere understanding, reading, and speculation."[29]

The roots theological symbols have in experience may help to account for the decided differences in theological affirmation among United Methodists. That difference is not in itself disturbing, but it becomes so when proponents of one perspective challenge another view's acceptability as a legitimately Christian position. To be sure, there would still be disagreement, even if every person in the denomination were to have similar experiences. But it is apparent that the differences of theological perspectives are exacerbated by the widely varying contexts in which different United Methodists live. Some parts of the church are in continuous contact with fellow United Methodists of different racial backgrounds and economic classes. Others maintain contact with church leaders in emerging Third World nations. In those contexts, theological symbols acquire meanings vitally connected with the situation they serve in and the active mission concerns that absorb them. Others are living out their faith in quite a different context. It is natural, therefore, that for this reason alone (and there are, of course, many other important reasons) there will be theological diversity in a large national denomination.

3. *Liturgy, Ritual as Symbolic Action.* A congregation's worship is central to its theology. In addition to rendering praise to God, an appropriate response of creatures to their Creator, worship is also a theological laboratory for the congregation. It is the context in which one acts out a certain stance toward life and toward God. By gesture, word, and action the worshiper declares something about life. The words of the Bible are used to illuminate the significance of what is happening in the daily round. The

events of life are lifted up as the substance of thanksgiving, confession, and intercession. United Methodists can hardly overstate the power of hymns to express the deepest convictions of the heart. Perhaps it is in our hymns that we find our most significant repository of theology.

Theology is undertaken in the midst of life, but it is in the worship and study of the congregation, as well as that of the home, that the images and attitudes are rehearsed and replenished. It is in the context of corporate worship that an understanding of the world as under the purposes of God is renewed and reinforced. In the sacrament of the Lord's Supper the whole congregation acts out its recollection of Christ, its hope for the future, its acceptance into God's people, and the members' sense of belonging to one another. All these symbolic acts are at the basis of one's theology. So formative is worship that it is difficult to distinguish sharply between the symbolic action of the people of God at worship and the action they engage in as they separate to go about their mission in the world. Both forms of action seek to acknowledge the reign of God and the extension of God's purposes among all people. Both allude to that which they cannot reduce to abstract propositions. It is not a truth they "have," but rather one that holds them through its power and conviction.

It is well known that we hold our view of the world together through rituals, whether secular or religious. Many have pointed out the ritualistic aspects of the Memorial Day observance in many of our towns, the football game, the cocktail party, the wedding, and a host of other social occasions. On such occasions, we engage in acts that reaffirm what we believe about the way things are. The Church provides a ritual by which we act out our understanding of the ultimate context of our lives. Worship seeks to interpret all of life in the light of the gospel. It thus reestablishes a world that is viewed under the love and mercy of God. It seeks to raise up hope, not the optimism that confirms our powers, but the transcendent hope rooted in the purposes and mercies of God.

The background of our denomination in revivalism should remind us of the theology that was acted out in the liturgy of the revival. In a revival, action often preceded understanding. The person hearing the proclamation of the Word was invited to respond to the action of God through Jesus Christ in a public action. That action was a public commitment, taken before persons who, in most cases, would see them during the week. The meaning of the walk to the altar was not neatly defined, but it indicated, through symbolic act, the intent of that person to make a decisive break with the past and to enter into a newly committed life.

Analysis of the elements of theology under the categories of feeling, thinking, and willing has been aimed partly at identifying points of divergence among theologies embraced by United Methodists. At the same time, we want to suggest that the point of entry into Christian faith and theological conviction may be found in any one of the elements noted. We have long been accustomed to the presentation of Christian faith in the form of biblical preaching, and this is, of course, central in the life of the Church. This analysis suggests, however, that some persons may be brought to theological conviction first through action or through renewed perception of what is happening in the world. If we are to be effective in commending Christian faith in our next century, we are going to have to learn to be as pluralistic in our methods as were the central actors in the Bible. There some heard God's good news as a verbal announcement. Others experienced it as buoyancy and strength in the course of obedience. Still others felt it as a new experience of the world viewed under God's grace. Theology in each instance was united to living faith by its involvement with the whole feeling, thinking, and willing individual.

# CHAPTER 5

# United Methodism, Faith, and the Future

We have sought in our discussion to show how a living theology provides guidance for, and in turn grows out of, a life of faithfulness. We have assumed that The United Methodist Church must find firm biblical and theological direction if it is to assume its full responsibility under God as it begins a third century of service in this world. When The United Methodist Church, or any denomination, receives its primary cues from understandings prevalent in the culture, without using the corrective of critical biblical and theological reflection, it really has nothing redemptive to say to the culture, and becomes merely a reflection of that culture.

But this abdication of responsibility *need* not—and we pray *will* not—be the case for Christians in the United Methodist tradition. There are important ways in which we share some of these critical concerns with large portions of the Christian church today, and in the foregoing pages we have sought to reflect that broad ecumenical concern. It is entirely appropriate, however, in thinking of our particular responsibilities in the context of the ecumenical Church, to accent some of those motifs that are a part of our heritage and that help equip us for an appropriate style of theology for the future. Our attempt in what follows will be, not to describe an official United Methodist theological position—even if that were possible—but to identify some authentic notes in our theological heritage that stand us in good stead for facing the days immediately ahead with faithfulness and theological integrity.

## A. Theological Motifs in United Methodist Traditions

1. *Theology and Its Practical Consequences.* The concerns of the formative figures in United Methodist theology were focused on the work of God in transforming lives and communities. Albright and Otterbein thought it more fitting to concentrate on conversion of men and women, than on abstract theological speculation.[1] Before them, John Wesley was urged by his mother, Susannah, to subordinate speculation to the practical venture of healing souls:

> Suffer now a word of advice. However curious you may be in searching into the nature, or in distinguishing the properties, of the passions or virtues of human kind, for your own private satisfaction, be very cautious in giving nice distinctions in public assemblies; for it does not answer the true end of preaching, which is to mend men's lives, and not fill their heads with unprofitable speculations.[2]

Wesley obviously agreed. When he wrote his preface to a printed collection of sermons, he stated that he was intending to write to the masses and not merely to those who were well-schooled. Those readers who were curious about speculative matters, he cautioned, had just as well save their time, for they would not find elegant or ornate language.

> I design plain truth for plain people: therefore, of set purpose, I abstain from all nice and philosophical speculations; from all perplexed and intricate reasonings; and, as far as possible, from even the show of learning, unless in sometimes citing the original Scripture.[3]

He therefore attempts "in some sense, to forget all that ever I have read in my life. I mean to speak, in the general, as if I had never read one author, ancient or modern: (always excepting the inspired)."[4]

Wesley's preaching, then, was aimed not so much to satisfy all the quandaries of the intellect as it was to heal the soul. Members of the earliest societies did not have to give their assent to certain doctrines. The one condition required for admission into the society was "a desire to flee from the wrath to come, to be saved from their sins."[5] Many years later, Wesley reiterated his intention to impose no "opinions" on those joining the societies. "One condition and one only, is required—A real desire to save their soul."[6] Wesley did not scorn the results of any human sphere of learning; he himself launched a formidable education movement. He nonetheless maintained the evangelistic and moral ends of the revival as the preeminent concern and designed the societies and bands to nurture the converted Christians in their new-found faith.

2. *Theology and the Experience of Faith.* The reality of the experience of assurance is a prominent motif in the theological traditions of The United Methodist Church. Otterbein and Albright expressed it as "justification by faith confirmed by a sensible assurance thereof. . . ."[7] Wesley likewise insisted that, even though we know of God through the natural order, that matters little unless there is an experience of God. Unless God opens our eyes, our knowledge of God is as removed from us as our knowledge of the Emperor of China.[8] Toward the end of his life, Wesley wrote that he had no fear about the continuation of the Methodist movement, but that he did fear lest it should continue having only the form of religion, without its power. And its power could be continued solely on the basis of a continuation of the practical experience of the

people, including doctrine, spirit, and discipline, established in the societies.[9]

There were those who criticized the Wesleyan revival because of the emotionalism, or "enthusiasm," as they called it, that accompanied their Methodist preaching services. Wesley disowned the charge of "enthusiast" and said that there was a rational basis for the religious faith he embodied and commended to others.[10] His brother, Charles, dealt decisively with extreme emotionalism. He was quite willing to accept the emotional reaction of persons who felt the burden of their sins lifted from them, but he recognized that there were some in his meetings who simply imitated the emotional outbursts of others. The shouts of some were so loud that he could barely be heard on some occasions. He once announced that anyone yelling out in an emotional reaction would be carried to a far corner of the room so that the rest could hear the preacher. Those whom he had asked to carry the emotional ones, he said, were idle all that evening.[11] Thus his emphasis on the heart was not a license for unbridled demonstration or for abandoning a rational examination of religious faith. It was, however, a means of suggesting that any religion with power will communicate through the heart, through the feelings, as well as through the mind.

3. *Faith and the Transformation of Life*. United Methodist theology has stressed that, although our obedience in no way earns or repays the mercy of God, the transformed life is a necessary mark of the redeemed life. Wesley related that the desire to be saved from one's sins was the sole requirement for entering the societies, but he promptly added that he expected that a pattern of living should evidence each person's continuing desire to be saved. Therefore, those who would be members of the societies were to do no harm, do good, and attend to the ordinances of God.[12] Under these three headings, directives were given which included avoidance of personal extravagance,

uncharitable conversation, giving or taking things on usury, etc. Positively, members of the societies were enjoined to give food to the hungry and to visit those who were sick or in prison. They were to deny themselves for the sake of the Gospel, to use their time intentionally, and to be frugal in their personal affairs.

While the focus of Wesley's attention was on the individual Christian who was converted and became a part of the Methodist movement, he also saw clearly the social dimensions of sin. In one of his writings, he traced the interconnected causes of poverty, outlining the relationship between the use of grain for distilling and the price of bread for the tables of the poor.[13] His hatred for the institution of slavery is well known. He incurred the enmity of influential people in the Georgia colony when, as a young missionary, he opposed the introduction of slavery into the colony.[14] Later, in a letter to William Wilberforce, the British statesman who crusaded against slavery and eventually succeeded in passing a bill in England abolishing the slave trade (1807), Wesley referred to slavery as "that execrable villany, which is the scandal of religion, of England, and of human nature." He concludes: "Go on, in the name of God and in the power of His might, till even American slavery (the vilest that ever saw the sun) shall vanish away before it."[15] For Wesley, a faithful, intentional life was so intimately related to the new birth that it was inconceivable that one could experience the latter and not lead the former.

4. *Expectation of Continuing Discovery.* Although John Wesley could be accused by no one of being reticent about expressing his views on matters he considered fundamental, his thought is remarkably free of doctrinal statements that would preclude further discovery and growth. Even in the controversies surrounding his preaching of perfection or entire sanctification, he took pains to point out that his understanding of perfection did not imply any exemption

from ignorance or mistake. It was rather the experience of
Christ living within the believer, enabling him or her to
love God fully and to manifest this love in life.[16] Whatever
else Christian perfection meant to Wesley, it was not a state
in which one had, in fixed form, the truth in its absolute
form. One pressed on to greater understanding, love, and
knowledge of God. And he urged the preachers to exhort
others to "go on to perfection," to "aspire after full
sanctification," conveying the sense of continuing discovery and growth.[17]

Wesley held that, on all matters not at the root of
Christianity, Methodists could "think and let think." He
encouraged them to attend to the forms of worship they
believed in, but to "beware of narrowness of spirit toward
those who use them not." They were urged also to examine
the doctrines to see which conformed to truth and reason,
but this was followed by the exhortation: "But have a care
of anger, dislike, or contempt toward those whose opinions
differ from yours."

> Condemn no man for not thinking as you think: let everyone
> enjoy the full and free liberty of thinking for himself; let every
> man use his own judgment, since every man must give an
> account of himself to God. Abhor every approach, in any kind
> of degree, to the spirit of persecution. If you cannot reason or
> persuade a man into the truth, never attempt to force him into
> it. If love will not compel him to come in, leave him to God, the
> Judge of all.[18]

Wesley commended a "catholic spirit" for his followers,
but such a spirit was in no way to be confused with
indifference in matters of belief, worship, or church polity.
The principal standard in all these matters was the Bible
itself. Wesley frequently referred to himself as a man of
one book.

> I believe all the Bible, as far as I understand it, and am ready to
> be convinced. If I am an heretic, I became such by reading the

Bible. All my notions I drew from thence. . . . But I impose my notions upon none: I will be bold to say, there is no man living farther from it. I make no opinion the term of union with any man: I think and let think. What I want is, holiness of heart and life. They who have this are my brother, sister, and mother.[19]

Next to the Scriptures, reason played a prominent role in continuing theological discovery. Wesley recognized the limits of reason, but he was anxious to show the detractors of the new movement that it was not without its basis in reason, as well as in experience. In his letter to Dr. Rutherford, he writes:

You go on: "It is a fundamental principle in the Methodist school that all who come into it must renounce their reason." Sir, are you awake? Unless you are talking in your sleep, how can you utter so gross an untruth? It is a fundamental principle with us that to renounce reason is to renounce religion, that religion and reason go hand and hand and that all irrational religion is false religion.[20]

Scriptures and reason, joined with tradition and the experience of God's grace in the life of the believer, formed the guides for a life of continuing growth and discovery in the riches of Christian faith.

## B. Doctrines and Authority
## in The United Methodist Church

The motifs of theology in the United Methodist tradition that we have just discussed are worthy guides from our past that should serve us well in developing theological perspectives for the future. In this matter, United Methodists have considerable freedom. The United Methodist Church has never adopted propositions of faith that every member of the church was obliged to accept. Instead of this "confessional" approach, United

Methodists have followed a conciliar principle, one that relies on the insights and understanding of members of the denomination for guidance in theology. For Wesley, Otterbein, and Albright, the conference provided the means by which each generation of Christians could reflect upon and decide the content of the Gospel that was to be proclaimed.

This is not to suggest that theology in the United Methodist tradition is without some guidelines and direction, however. John Wesley provided four volumes of sermons (written 1746–1760), *Sermons on Several Occasions*, and a brief commentary on the Scriptures, *Explanatory Notes upon the New Testament* (1754), which were included in the 1763 "Model Deed" for the chapels. The Deed provided that duly appointed Methodist preachers should be allowed to use the chapels, "provided always, that the said persons preach no other doctrine than is contained in Mr. Wesley's *Notes upon the New Testament* and four volumes of *Sermons*."[21] The Constitution of The United Methodist Church contains the restriction that the General Conference shall not "revoke, alter, or change our Articles of Religion or establish any new standards or rules of doctrine contrary to our present existing and established standards of doctrine."[22] Those articles were the ones that, with some amendments, had first been sent to the colonies by John Wesley in 1784. A section of the Discipline outlines the usage for standards of doctrine as it was developed in the former Methodist and in the former Evangelical United Brethren churches.[23]

But these doctrinal standards have been interpreted as "landmarks" along the path of continuing discovery, rather than as shrines before which succeeding generations must worship. They are to be taken with seriousness, but to be interpreted in their historical context. They are not to be a condition of membership in the denomination.

In addition to the landmark documents, The United

Methodist Church has acknowledged the continuing guidance of four norms for testing the adequacy of Christian theology: Scripture, tradition, reason, and experience. And it has encouraged the whole church to engage in theological reflection as a right and appropriate challenge for all Christians.[24] Commendation of these norms suggests that the work of theology is a continuing task of the Church, never to be summed up in final and definitive form. So long as the Church continues to proclaim the Gospel and to translate its message into concrete deeds of justice and compassion, there will be new data to be discovered and new light to be shed on the meaning of Christian faith for each generation.

The four norms are to be understood in their interdependence, not in isolation. The Bible, however, occupies a primary place as the source of authority in theology. It is, in the Discipline's words, "the primitive source of the memories, images, and hopes by which the Christian community came into existence and that still confirm and nourish its faith and understanding."[25] To embrace *Scriptures* as a primary standard for our theology is to acknowledge that, in the events recounted therein, we find the determinative clues about the meaning of our lives. Since Jesus Christ is the center of the biblical revelation, other events of the Bible are interpreted through their relationship to him.

To understand the Bible as a witness to God's self-revelation allows United Methodists to heed the primary authority of the biblical witness, and at the same time, to avoid a narrow literalism in approaching its pages. It acknowledges that the determinative authority is in God's own acts, and that the human witnesses to those events, while inspired, are still subject to the fallibility that mortal flesh is heir to. Such a stance encourages Christians to listen for the Word of God in the pages of the Bible and to employ the best critical methods available for understanding its meaning for their time and our own.

Identification of *tradition* as an authority in Christian theology is a recognition of the fact that Christian theology has taken shape from its origins and through the living faith of each generation. It was out of the earliest traditions that significant portions of the Bible were formed, and it is partly out of the study and proclamation of each generation that our current understanding of the Bible is formed. Each generation of Christians has sought to express the truth of faith in terms appropriate to its own situation. We are free, and obliged, to learn from their discovery. We should not assume that a new idea, by virtue of its newness, is superior in its insight to the old.

But the enterprise of discovery every serious Christian is engaged in is one that requires the use of *reason,* as well as Scripture and tradition. To believe the Christian message is to believe not only that it offers personal satisfactions, but that it is true, and deserves to be recognized as such. Reason is the facility of the human mind for relating one element of experience to another, comparing critically what we know through one area of life with what we know through other areas. Reason is employed in the communication of the Gospel, phrasing its message in the most cogent, thoughtful terms the believer is capable of.

We should neither claim too much, nor settle for too little, when talking about the role of reason in our understanding of faith. The truth of Christian faith cannot be encapsulated in the categories of reason. But recognition of the limits of reason does not excuse the serious Christian from the duty of weighing claims to truth seriously, and employing reason to the limits of her or his ability, in determining the most adequate means of phrasing the truth as he or she has encountered it.

Finally, for any of these norms to have significance, their force must be confirmed in our own *experience.* Obviously, there is no truth we can be aware of that does not come to us through the medium of our own experience. The most direct revelation could be acknowledged as revelation only by someone who experienced it as such. Theological understanding is an ongoing venture of discovery precisely because we are learning more about God, the self, and the world through all our experiences.

If we have identified any problem in theology among contemporary United Methodists, as well as in the wider circle of Christian believers, it is the serious split between their everyday experience and their theological convictions. To treat Christian faith as self-validating assertions that need not be treated in experience will not overcome this serious split. The truths commended in Christian faith must constantly be placed beside our actual experience and thus tested for their adequacy and force in our lives. Theology comes alive when biblical terms help us interpret our experience, and our experience in turn helps us grasp the meaning of biblical terms.

## C. Recurring Questions and Changing Forms

But what of the future of theological reflection? There are doubtless many Christians who question, at least occasionally, whether faith has a future. Forces within the environment that challenge theology, as we noted in chapter 2, are obvious to any sensitive person today. But the burden of our discussion has been to suggest that theological questions are at the center of life. They plunge beneath the superficial quandaries of life and bring us face-to-face with the most basic and radical questions of our lives. Theological symbols embody our most inclusive hopes for life; they clothe and nourish our most fundamental reliance on the trustworthiness of that Ultimate Reality with whom every man or woman must struggle. Theological questions, therefore, do not disappear. In a period of rapid change, they may become camouflaged, in one season under the cover of technology, and in another under the guise of personal adjustment and fulfillment, but they do not go away. For the sake of our full humanity, to say nothing of our responsibility for proclaiming the Gospel, it is necessary for the Church to persist in raising the fundamental theological questions, which are not peripheral but fundamental to human life. To replace these basic questions with less profound ones is to trivialize life, to betray its most fundamental intuitions.

But if theological questions do not disappear, they certainly do assume different shapes in different historical epochs. When the people of Israel entered into the Promised Land, they confronted there a host of new issues and problems. Accustomed to the life of following the herds, they now confronted the challenge of earning their livelihood by tilling the soil. It was not at all apparent to them that the Jahweh who had led them faithfully through the wilderness way held sway over the fertility of the fields in which they labored. Those who inhabited the land sought to assure the fruitfulness of their fields by devotion to the fertility gods. This new situation prompted a theological-ethical crisis for the people of Israel. The new gods seemed to be the force actually in control in this strange new land, so they attempted to combine worship of Jahweh with devotion to the new gods of the land. And it was the task of the prophets to insist that, though their situation was new, the basic questions of faith were still the same: Were they to serve Jahweh who had entered into covenant with them and faithfully kept the divine promise, or were they faithlessly to follow those who really were not gods, and thus betray their rightful Lord? And the stakes for upholding or betraying the covenant were life or ruin. The prophets were given to see the recurring nature of the questions they faced in the midst of changing forms.

The contemporary world likewise puts us before a

cluster of problems and issues we have not faced in their present forms. In the midst of these quandaries are entrancing new powers that are thought by some to be the deliverers of tomorrow. Recognizing these new quandaries, many people conclude that the God trusted in the past to deal with these problems is no longer appropriate for the modern world. Faced with a staggering sense of responsibility for the world, yet cut off from active trust in faithful purpose, contemporary men and women are tempted to place their confidence in a host of surrogate gods—technologies, ideologies, self-help schemes, hedonism, nation-states, or military force. The theological danger of our time is not that we will have no God, but that we will have far too many gods!

The Church is faced with a prophetic task at this turning point in history. It is a part of the mission of the Church to discern the changing forms in which the perennial questions of human life are raised. The origins of United Methodism were in a passionate desire to be forgiven for one's sins and to be delivered from the "wrath to come." It is apparent that the reality of sin is just as oppressive a force today as it was in the time of Wesley, Otterbein, and Albright. Neither has the apprehension of a wrath to come—whether within or beyond history—disappeared from the lives of people. One need not be a cynic to note that breakthroughs that promise to ease human suffering and benefit the human race have a corresponding capacity to serve the greed of the few and to inflict poverty and misery on the many.

An adroit, theologically alive church will know how to interpret the meaning of the times we are passing through. It will be able to discern the deeper questions of spirit that underlie the topical concerns of our contemporaries. It will be able to articulate the recurring questions, even in the midst of their changing forms.

One example of this adroitness and discernment is

found in Paul Tillich's description of the basic experience of anxiety. Anxiety, for him, is not a pathological state, but an intrinsic element in the human situation. It is the threat to our being represented by the force of *nonbeing*. Nonbeing, says Tillich, threatens our attempts to affirm our own being. In relative terms it appears as fate; in absolute terms it is *death*. When we seek to affirm our spiritual being, nonbeing lurks in its relative form as emptiness, and in absolute form it is known as *meaninglessness*. And when we seek to affirm ourselves morally, we find anxiety immediately at hand in the form of guilt. In absolute terms, we experience it as *condemnation*. These three expressions of anxiety—death, meaninglessness, and condemnation—all bespeak the struggle of the human being with the force of nonbeing which threatens his or her existence.[26]

Furthermore, says Tillich, periods of anxiety in Western history are most prominent at times when one period of history is breaking up and another is in formation. The type of anxiety that was most visible at the breakup of the ancient period of history was the anxiety about fate and *death*. Later, at the dissolution of the Middle Ages, persons experienced anxiety in the form of guilt, or absolute *condemnation*. They mounted pilgrimages, paid indulgences, devoted themselves to relics, and participated in a host of practices to deliver themselves from the wrath they believed would befall them for their sins. The proclamation that God's free grace justifies and sanctifies the sinner represented marvelous good news to a person laboring under anxiety experienced as condemnation.[27] This proclamation brought the relief a sleeper feels who awakens from a nightmare and finds that the peril that loomed so devastatingly only a moment before is now no more. And it was in this message that United Methodism had its birth.

In our time, continues Tillich, we are living in a third period of anxiety, the anxiety of emptiness or absolute *meaninglessness.* Many lack a core interpretive principle that would connect experience in a coherent, significant whole. Life presents itself as disjointed, chaotic, dissonant, and signifying nothing. This experience of meaninglessness is frequently portrayed in contemporary art forms with their clashing colors, nonrepresentative forms, dissonant sounds, absence of a plot, and other absurdist's techniques.

It would clearly be wrong to think that emptiness and meaninglessness have replaced guilt and condemnation as the only form in which the question of salvation appears. Preoccupation with finding meaning and with speaking to the nonbeliever is doubtless partly a reflection of our Western context. Latin American Christians have been reminding us that the problem they face in the midst of grinding poverty and economic exploitation is not that of the nonbeliever but that of the nonperson, "the poor, the exploited, the one systematically deprived of being a person, the one who scarcely knows that he is a person." For them, then, the question is "not how to announce God in an adult world; but rather how to announce Him as Father in a nonhuman world."[28]

It is appropriate to ask ourselves the manner and forms in which basic questions of salvation and liberation are being raised among people in our country and in other nations today. The church that is genuinely a movement, and not merely an institution, will enter imaginatively into people's questions, expecting to find, not questions to which an automatic answer may be provided, but issues that will help the church itself probe more deeply into the meaning of salvation and liberation in the name of Jesus Christ.

The church would be faithless were it to reduce the living Gospel to a formula that would require people to phrase their innermost needs in the same terms as those used by the Wesleys and their followers. We would do well

to learn from Jesus' own proclamation of the coming New
Age, or the kingdom of God. His ministry represented the
shock of the New Age confronting the powers of the old.
He encountered the old order, however, in a number of
forms. For some, the inevitabilities of the old order
expressed themselves in physical sickness. For others they
were sickness in spirit, or possession by demons. Other
persons were oppressed by the sin of the old order or by a
social and economic standing that branded them sinners.
Jesus addressed people with the promise of the New Age in
their own situation, not demanding that they express
themselves in an established formula before the New Age
could come among them in power. If we believe that God is
alive and is working out the divine purposes in the
contemporary situation, then we must be trusting enough
to enter into the life of the world, confident that we will
find God's redeeming power in the midst of life in
marvelous and unexpected ways. Least of all can we divide
life into false and misleading categories, presuming to limit
God's work to spiritual affairs and to matters of personal
morality. If God is Creator, Redeemer, and Sustainer of all
life, then God's saving power cannot be confined to spirit in
opposition to the body, or to the sphere of religion to the
denigration of politics or economics, or to the individual as
opposed to the social order. Faith in the living God
requires that we be prepared to hear the recurring
questions of the human spirit in the multitude of forms
they are likely to take.

# CHAPTER 6

# Renewal of Theology Among United Methodists

Portions of the preceding chapter reviewed principal motifs in United Methodist theological perspectives which will be worthy guides in the century ahead. We give our attention in this concluding chapter to some of the qualities we believe are necessary if The United Methodist Church is to find renewed theological vitality and clarity in its message and ministry in the years to come.

## A. Reference to a Context

A context is "the interrelated conditions in which something exists or occurs."[1] The interrelated conditions for theology represent every element of life. They relate to a renewed perception or experience of life, a set of images and stories life is organized by, theories that articulate one's elemental perception of the world, and a series of enacted models—liturgy and mission—that put one's theology into action.

It is in the context of historical events that the name "God" acquires meaning. The Bible does not begin with a set of definitions and proofs. It tells the story of a people who, in the circumstances of their lives and all that they underwent, were encountered by God. We receive their witness as we hear again the story of how God acted in the context of a historical community. Each actor in the drama of the Bible lives out his or her story as an episode in a larger story. Therefore, when each witness encounters God in her or his life, it is not as if this were an entirely new happening. It is, rather, a continuation of the story that began in the garden and continued through generation after generation. When each successive generation encountered that overwhelming reality in their lives, they did not identify it with a local deity but with the Name they had heard from their mothers and fathers.[2]

As each generation enters the context of risk and decision, of struggle and hope, of forgiveness and new life, it learns to identify the realities of its context through what it has learned from the testimony of others in similar circumstances. When we, as persons or in communities, come face-to-face with the utter limits of life, confronting that Ultimate Reality from whom we cannot escape, then the name of God, as it has been learned through the traditions of others, takes on vitality and force in our lives. To face the cutting, ragged edges of life—for example, the loss through death of a spouse, a son or daughter, a lifelong friend—and yet to trust and love God is to invest that name with significance and meaning for our lives. Or to find ourselves completely condemned by the standards we acknowledge to be right and just, to see ourselves bereft of any means of self-justification, and yet to know in this extremity that the pain of our faithlessness is received and that through grace we can still live—this is a great benediction that makes the love of God tangible and real in the context of our lives. To be moved beyond words by the beauty of human love and by all things sublime and magnificent in the created order, and to receive all these benefits as disclosure of the One who is far more even than these great gifts, is to know in the most intimate terms of our lives the magnificence and the beauty of God.

All this is intended to suggest that it is in the context of our living, our feeling, thinking, and willing, that the terms of theology come to life and help us structure our most fundamental responses to life. The categories of theology are employed aright when they help us form our basic perspectives and dispositions toward life. To have faith in Christ is to embody a fundamental predisposition of trust toward life, a trust in the goodness of God and a hope for the future. To have faith in Christ is to possess a fundamental intention toward life, a basic orientation and direction one is moved to pursue in the context of all that one undergoes.[3]

In living theology, the deeds of God witnessed to in the Bible are reduplicated in the life of the believer. To have known betrayal and abandonment is to know something about the sting of the cross. To have been raised up out of defeat and abandonment and find the capacity to live fully again is to know something about resurrection. To have cared deeply about God's human family and to have persisted in hope and struggle to give it political and economic expression despite formidable odds, is to have fundamental involvement in theological categories of Creation and Christian hope. While no one would elect for oneself or for another to undergo suffering and imprisonment, it is striking to see how clear the categories of Christian faith become to those who are denied every other means of support, and who experience, in the context of their own extremity, the great realities of faith.

If Christian faith is intended for our practical guidance, then we should not be surprised that our theological insights fade when they lose touch with the contexts and practices they are associated with in history. Jesus himself connected comprehension of his teaching with the life of discipleship: "If you continue in my word, you are truly my disciples, and you will know the truth, and the truth will make you free" (John 8:31-32). The pathway to theological renewal leads directly through the context of mission and commitment.

## B. Focus upon the Future

Attentiveness to the context in which contemporary
men and women live their lives requires that the Church
address the question of the future in explicitly theological
terms. Theology as our speech about God has always dealt
with transcendence; that is, that which surpasses or goes
beyond our ordinary experience. Typically, the quality of
transcendence in Christian history has been understood in
spatial terms. In traditional language, we speak of God and
heaven as *above* the earth. Salvation, therefore, possesses a
spatial form; to be saved is to be delivered from the earth,
which is below, to the higher realm of heaven. In other
words, the realm above is the spatial expression for that
which goes beyond our ordinary experience, for that over
which we have no control, and therefore that which fills us
with awe, apprehension, or hope.

The use of spatial expressions for transcendence is in no
way to be scorned; any human speech about God will, of
necessity, employ terms drawn out of our own experience
to describe what essentially goes beyond that experience.
But we should recognize that the means of expressing
transcendence, for many of our contemporaries, is
shifting from spatial terms to temporal terms; that is, time,
history, and the future. Whenever the times people live in
are fragile and tenuous, there is a renewed focus on the
future as the realm that fills people with a sense of
fascination, awe, dread, optimism, or hope. Such a focus is
now quite apparent in our secular, as well as in our
theological, expressions of concern. Secular prophets
regularly ask in our newspapers, magazines, and books
whether the world can be saved from the threats now
looming over it. The disciplined study of the future has
found its way into university curricula. With increasing
frequency, we are offered observations on the shape things
will assume in the year 2,000.

It is at least arguable, therefore, that if speech about God concerns itself with that which goes beyond our experience, the realm of transcendence that is gripping and compelling for contemporary women and men is the future. For it is in that realm that they confront most imaginatively that over which they have no control, that which is filled with awe and dread or with promise and potential.

Humans frequently respond to concerns for the future by attempting to return to origins. It is assumed by some that a primitive state of bliss existed before the advent of time, and by escaping time and returning to that state of bliss, one may be saved. Religions frequently embody symbols for origins and for rebirth of the individual. In experiencing rebirth, the believer at least temporarily overcomes the oppressiveness of time and is restored to a blissful state.

We should note that there are evidences of this approach to time and the future throughout the biblical witness and in subsequent history. The prophets inveighed against the form of the return motif that emphasized returning to the elemental forces of nature through fertility worship and sacred prostitution (thinking to gain control thereby over the process of reproduction in field and flocks). Some secular salvation schemes stress return to origins, even if in quite different terms. Sigmund Freud, for example, assumes we originally existed in a blissful state long before the forces of repression and guilt affected us. Psychoanalysis, therefore, is, among other things, a way of confronting those events that generated our neuroses and psychoses and thereby of gaining a measure of mastery over them. Even the Marxist salvation myth, oriented as it is to concrete change in historical circumstances, aims at the recreation of a primitive society in which all the oppressive forces generated through history are undone.[4]

It scarcely needs to be added that in the face of great

apprehension about the future, some forms of Christian proclamation stress the return and rebirth motifs in a manner that makes them quite compatible with the non-Christian and secular salvation myths we have just alluded to. In many forms of contemporary mysticism, salvation is represented as a process by which one, at least spiritually, absents oneself from history and focuses on a heavenly state, which is one's real "home." The historical circumstances and the historical movements surrounding one are, at best, insignificant to the state of one's soul, and more frequently are regarded as trials or distractions from that primary interest.

To represent Christian salvation in such terms requires that one struggle against some of the plainest expressions of Scripture, for it is obvious throughout the Scriptures that God was involved in the intimate affairs of history and was not known save through history. Truth, in the Bible, was not confined to an isolated sphere outside of history; truth was something that happened.[5] This was the reason that Jahweh was described, not through propositions, but through narrative and story. Only the recital of decisive events could witness adequately to the Reality known through the medium of history.

Reinhold Niebuhr has reminded us of the decisive difference christological expectation makes between religions and philosophies of history in which no Christ is expected, and the faith in which a Christ is expected. A history in which Christ is expected is one, as Niebuhr put it, in which "history is regarded as potentially meaningful but as still awaiting the full disclosure and fulfillment of its meaning."[6] For Christian faith, Christ is the "midpoint of history" in the deepest meaning of that expression. Christ is the decisive self-disclosure of God's being and purpose, and every year before and after that event bears a numerical as well as a spiritual relationship to it.[7] To call Jesus "Christ" is to confess that, in him, in his life, death, and resurrection, the ultimate intent of history has appeared in the midst of time.

Though "we do not yet see everything in subjection to him" (Heb. 2:8b), we live in confidence that the last syllable of history will confirm what we have learned to hope for through faith in him. The hope of God's final victory, a victory already anticipated in God's raising of Jesus from the dead, is what fuels history with possibility and promise. Therefore, the future is not simply the result of inevitable forces coming out of the past; it is the reality that lures what is to come out of what now is.

It is in this significant sense, then, that it is accurate to say that the future determines the past. For, when we are sustained in hope, our view of the future is inevitably colored by our expectation of novelty and surprise in the future. When we read the sacred story of the past, it is not to return to those originating events and thus escape history; rather, it is to root ourselves in the hope that is nourished by God's doings in the past and the divine promises for the future.

Hope of the sort we refer to is not merely an optimistic reading of events that is derived from a careful weighing of the odds. It goes beyond optimism and pessimism. As Colin Morris suggested, pessimism makes hope seem impossible; optimism makes it unnecessary.[8]

Hope for the future as a means of invigorating our expectancy for the present and giving us heart to continue the struggle against impossible odds is a natural inheritance for the Christian. Christian theology should welcome the focus on the future that is so apparent just now, for the future is the Christian's native soil! And it is in delivering the future from the sense of fatalism that so many sense that Christian theology may make one of its most redeeming contributions. It is a desperate feeling to know that the present order of things cannot continue indefinitely, and yet feel confronted with formidable obstacles to any desired change. It is far more desperate to sense the breakup of present arrangements for the world and still feel trapped and seduced by its assumptions. Many people know that the world cannot continue with its expanding chasms between wealth and poverty. They know that we cannot continue to envision the future simply as the multiplication of the goods that invest the present. Indeed, many are now, for the first time, sensing that the future will promise them less, rather than more, of the consumer goods they have customarily seen as a part of the "good life." But, although they sense that present circumstances will be changed, they cannot find it within themselves to imagine any state of affairs preferable to the present.

Like the people who followed Moses, we often experience the possibility of liberation, not as freedom, but as death (see Exod. 14:11-12). Like them, we are tempted to plead for the slavery of the past in preference to the place of promise that lies before us. The prophetic task for Moses and for persons of faith today is to live by an alternative future, one that is determined, not by ironclad rules of predictability inherited from the past, but by the freedom of God who has pledged us a future. Just when the world has resigned itself to the futility its greed and "warring madness" lead it to, the church may be blessed with the grace to proclaim other possibilities founded on promises of God disclosed in the face of Jesus Christ.

At the very time when we United Methodists begin our third century of ministry and witness in this nation, we are confronted with an unusual preoccupation among our contemporaries with the future. A theology that is pertinent to the present and faithful to its past will focus on the authentic hope that is indigenous to the Gospel, and the alternative possibilities and visions that spring from that hope. The God who is the power of the future itself can yet fulfill the divine promises amidst the wastes and desolations we have wrought in our history. The farmer in

Jesus' parable of the sower was the one who flung away the security of the grain in his hand—all that was predictable and tangible—and invested in the precarious promise of the harvest. And Jesus said that joining the New Age was comparable to such a risk-filled venture. A renewed theology is linked with life that is invested in the future of God.

## C. Identification with the Dispossessed

Historically it has been primarily those who live on the margins of life, those who can find no "affirmation," as we term it, by the customary arrangements, who have heard and heeded the promises of the New Age. It is not because they are necessarily morally superior to others that this is the case. They simply find nothing in the present arrangements to give them hope. To believe that God is free and sovereign in history to fulfill the divine promises fuels them with hope for a better state of affairs. On the other hand, those who fare well with the existing order frequently interpret the future not as a promise at all, but as a threat. Jesus' debates with the Pharisees, some of the most earnest religious people of his day, are obvious examples of this.

There are many pressing reasons pointing to the need for the Church to identify with the dispossessed in this land and throughout the world. The Church can hardly be a sign of a renewed and redeemed humanity if it simply reflects the tragic divisions between nationalities, races, and economic groups that already plague the planet. Strictly speaking, a "church" that mirrors the most oppressive divisions of the world is a contradiction in terms.

In order to have theological integrity—to say nothing of other equally compelling reasons—we of the Church need a sturdy identification with those who are dispossessed. If our discussion of theology has demonstrated anything, it is that the theological views we espouse are intimately related to our context. A theology forged exclusively in masculine terms, singularly in the context of the white community, or dominantly from the perspective of Western industrialized society, will inevitably be a warped version of Christian faith. If we wish to transcend the divisions of our society and the biases that are a part of our situation then it is indispensable that we develop a genuinely inclusive church, one that cares enough about authentic pluralism to struggle on until, by the grace of God, every shred of racism, nationalism, and sexism is overcome.

The relative affluence of the Western industrialized nations is experienced by a comparatively small number of the earth's people. It is difficult to believe in the God of justice and yet be indifferent to the massive suffering imposed upon two-thirds of the world to maintain a luxurious standard of living for the rest of us. If we are to hear what God is saying to us, if we are to learn the things that make for peace and justice, then we need to heed the voices of Christians and persons of other faiths who most directly experience the inequities and injustices of the present order. Perhaps those in this land who have experienced oppression and prejudice most concretely, particularly persons of minority racial and ethnic groups, can lead us most effectively in appropriating a faith that is pertinent to a world that must be transformed, or perish. It is, therefore, in the interests of the whole Church, and the humanity it seeks to serve, to strengthen the voices of ethnic minority persons in our churches. It would not be the first time in history that the victim became the teacher and the healer. A theology that is adequate for the time immediately ahead will be, of necessity, a genuinely pluralistic theology.

## D. Pathways to Theological Renewal

The theological uncertainty we observe in various sectors is more a symptom than a root cause of some of our current problems. Theological renewal awaits remedies in sectors of the Church, some of which are outside the formal study of theology itself. It does not diminish the importance of theological research to suggest that a vital theology is linked with a compelling sense of mission on the part of the Church. If there is to be theological renewal in the Church, it will come as part of a similar renewal in action, in our mission and worship, in our perception of the world, and in our appropriation of biblical symbols and images, as well as in our theological doctrines. When we participate in the agonies of this world with the force of Christian hope, confident that what God has declared in the death and the rising again of Christ will, in the last day, be vindicated for all to see, we lay claim on the full force of Christian faith and Christian theology.

Persons who fasten onto a new purpose in their history find it necessary to recapture the parts of their history that are relevant to their new intent. When a country has a revolution, it changes the list of heroes in its history. Similarly, when we give ourselves to the new world that God has promised in Christ and that is appearing in glimpses and intimations (or as "foretastes" or "first fruits," as Paul calls them), we likewise grasp anew the significance of Scripture. The words come alive. The issues of theology come upon us with new moment. They are no longer merely answers to speculative questions, but life-and-death insights necessary for us and for the practical regulation of our lives.

Faithfulness in Christian life does not await full disclosure of all mysteries; instead, it awaits our faithfully acting upon what we already know. As we give ourselves to the vision in Christ of a renewed humanity, we will be given the light necessary to walk ahead in faithfulness.

In the meantime, we represent in liturgy our hope and our present agony for the coming fulfillment of that hope. We confess before God and one another our betrayal of the hope. We offer ourselves symbolically on behalf of all. We hear the ancient Word and the contemporary Word spoken in the midst of life. We represent, through the Lord's Supper, the Table which has appeared once and will appear again in the Last Day. That Table, hosted by God, is the promised place where, all appearances in the present notwithstanding, all God's children will come together at last. None will be in want. All will belong. When we act in that faith and strive to give substance to present signs of its coming, we are already in the path that leads to continuing discovery of the truth of God.

> He is the Way.
> Follow Him through the
>     Land of Unlikeness;
> you will see rare beasts,
>     and have unique adventures.
>
> He is the Truth.
> Seek Him in the Kingdom of Anxiety;
> you will come to a great city that has
>     expected your return for years.
>
> He is the Life.
> Love Him in the World of the Flesh;
> and at your marriage all its occasions
>     shall dance for joy.[9]

# Notes

## Chapter 1

1. *Luther's Large Catechism,* trans. J. N. Lenker (Minneapolis: Augsburg Publishing House, 1967), p. 10.
2. Paul Tillich, *Systematic Theology,* vol. 1 (Chicago: University of Chicago Press, 1951), p. 12.
3. William E. Ramsden, *The Church in a Changing Society* (Nashville: Abingdon, 1980), p. 46.
4. *The United Methodist Reporter,* March 30, 1979.
5. *The Book of Discipline of The United Methodist Church* (Nashville: The United Methodist Publishing House, 1980), pp. 49-50. Referred to hereafter as the Discipline.
6. *Ibid.,* p. 73.
7. *Ibid.*
8. Terms suggested by Jurgen Moltmann in his *The Crucified God,* trans. R. A. Wilson and John Bowden (New York: Harper & Row, 1974), chapter 1.
9. Heinrich Ott, *God* (Richmond: John Knox Press, 1974), p. 106.
10. A report of *Zion's Herald,* May, 1980.
11. Moltmann, *The Crucified God,* p. 16.
12. Ramsden, *The Church in a Changing Society,* p. 11.
13. *Ibid.,* p. 19.
14. *Ibid.,* pp. 25 f.
15. John S. Simon, *John Wesley and the Methodist Societies,* lst ed. (London: Epworth Press, 1923), pp. 101 ff.
16. John Wesley, "A Plain Account of the People Called Methodists," in *The Works of the Rev. John Wesley, A.M.,* 11th ed. (London: John Mason, 1856), VIII, p. 240.
17. See his sermon "Catholic Spirit" in *Wesley's Standard Sermons,* 4th ed. (London: Epworth Press, 1956), II, pp. 126-46.

18. James Broughton, "The Last Word: Or, What to Say About It," in *Religious Drama 3,* ed. Marvin Halverson (New York: Meridian Books, 1959), pp. 17-28. Used by permission.

19. Peter Berger, *The Heretical Imperative* (Garden City: Anchor Press, 1979). While it is phrased in different terms, the author is indebted to the discussion of contemporary theological positions in the Berger volume cited.

20. Douglas Rennick and James Shelton, unpublished paper for Metropolitan Urban Service and Training (MUST), New York, N.Y. Quoted in Neal Fisher, "Where on Earth Do You 'Do Theology'?" *Christian Century* (October 28, 1970), p. 1293.

21. Berger, *The Heretical Imperative,* p. xiii.

## Chapter 2

1. William R. Taylor, Exegesis on Psalm 53, in *The Interpreter's Bible,* vol. 4, ed. George Buttrick (New York: Abingdon Press, 1955), p. 278.

2. *Ibid.*

3. See this emphasis in Robert Bellah, *Beyond Belief* (New York: Harper & Row, 1970), pp. 216 f.

4. In the discussion that follows, the author has drawn in important ways upon the organization of the forms of atheism in S. Paul Schilling's, *God in an Age of Atheism* (New York: Abingdon Press, 1969), esp. chapter 3, pp. 115-34.

5. See the summary discussion of this view in Adolfo Sanchez Vazquez, *The Philosophy of Praxis,* trans. Mike Gonzalez (Atlantic Highlands, N.J.: Humanities Press, 1977), pp. 70-71.

6. *Ibid.,* p. 76.

7. *Ibid.,* p. 81.

8. Ludwig Feuerbach, *The Essence of Christianity,* trans. George Eliot (New York: Harper & Brothers, 1957), p. 184.

9. See Wolfhart Pannenberg, *The Idea of God and Human Freedom,* trans. R. A. Wilson (Philadelphia: The Westminster Press, 1973), pp. 86 f.

10. Vazquez, *Philosophy of Praxis,* pp. 120 f.

11. *Ibid.,* p. 125.

12. Karl Marx, "Contribution to the Critique of Hegel's Philosophy of Right," in *On Religion* (New York: Scholken Books, 1964), p. 42.

13. *Ibid.*

14. See this summary in Ana-Maria Rizzuto, *The Birth of the*

*Living God* (Chicago: University of Chicago Press, 1979), p. 15.

15. Sigmund Freud, *The Future of an Illusion*, trans. James Strachey (New York: W. W. Norton & Co., 1961), pp. 42 f., 49 f.

16. *Ibid.*, pp. 40 f., 50.

17. *Ibid.*, pp. 42 f., 49.

18. *Ibid.*, pp. 32-33.

19. Rizzuto, *Birth of the Living God*, p. 209.

20. See Gordon Kaufman, *God the Problem* (Cambridge: Harvard University Press, 1972), p. 13.

21. John Wilson, *Language and Christian Faith* (New York: St. Martin's Press, 1958), pp. xi-xii.

22. Frederick Ferré, *Language, Logic and God* (New York: Harper & Brothers, 1961), pp. 9-15.

23. Antony Flew and Alasdair MacIntyre, eds., *New Essays in Philosophical Theology* (New York: The Macmillan Co., 1955).

24. Quoted in Mary Daly, *Beyond God the Father* (Boston: Beacon Press, 1973), p. 1.

25. See Peter L. Berger and Thomas Luckmann, *The Social Construction of Reality: A Treatise in the Sociology of Knowledge* (Garden City, N.Y.: Doubleday & Co., 1966 [1967]), p. 61.

26. See Ernest Becker, *The Birth and Death of Meaning* (New York: The Macmillan Co., 1962), p. 52.

27. Karl Rahner's discussion may be found in his *Inquiries* (New York: Herder and Herder, 1964), pp. 403-63. Dulles discusses the idea in an unpublished paper, "The Hartford Appeal and Ecumenism," presented at Hartford, Connecticut, March 5, 1975.

28. A discussion of this idea may be found in Peter Berger's earlier *The Sacred Canopy* (Garden City, N.Y.: Doubleday & Co., 1969); and in his more recent *The Heretical Imperative* (Garden City, N.Y.: Anchor Press, 1979). See also *The Social Construction of Reality* (New York: Irvington Publishers, 1966).

29. Berger, *The Heretical Imperative*, p. 18.

30. *Ibid.*, p. 11.

31. *Ibid.*, p. 28.

32. See these conclusions in James T. Borhek and Richard F. Curtis, *The Sociology of Belief* (New York: John Wiley & Sons, 1975), pp. 97-107.

33. Langdon Gilkey, "Dissolution and Reconstruction in Theol-

ogy," in *Frontline Theology*, ed. Dean Peerman (Richmond, Va.: John Knox Press, 1967), p. 31.

34. The following discussion draws in important ways upon Langdon Gilkey, *Naming the Whirlwind: The Renewal of God-Language* (Indianapolis: Bobbs-Merrill, 1969), pp. 40-71.

35. *Ibid.*, p. 53.

36. Thomas Kuhn, *The Structures of Scientific Revolutions* (Chicago: University of Chicago Press, 1970).

37. See Willis W. Harman's *An Incomplete Guide to the Future* (San Francisco: The San Francisco Book Company, 1976), pp. 24-37.

38. *Ibid.*, p. 38.

39. See Herbert W. Richardson, *Toward an American Theology* (New York: Harper & Row, 1967), especially chapter 4.

40. Lester Brown, "The Discontinuities Before Us," *The Futurist* (June, 1975), pp. 122-31.

41. For more on the implications of such terms, see Daniel Bell, *The Coming of the Post-Industrial Society* (New York: Basic Books, 1973), pp. 51-53.

42. Harman, *An Incomplete Guide to the Future*, p. 117. The last item cited was included in his "Key Choices of the Next Two Decades: An Exploration of the Future," in *Fields Within Fields . . . Within Fields: The Methodology of Pattern*, ed. Julius Stulman (New York: World Institute Council, 1972), p. 87.

43. Richardson, *Toward an American Theology*, pp. 4-5.

44. *Ibid.*, p. 5.

45. For changes in Israel's basic paradigms as they changed from nomadic people to farming people, see Gerhard von Rad, *Old Testament Theology*, vol. 1, *The Theology of Israel's Historical Traditions*, trans. D. M. G. Stalker (New York: Harper & Row, Publishers, 1962), pp. 15-35.

46. Jose Miguez Bonino, *Christians and Marxists* (Grand Rapids: Eerdmans Publishing Co., 1976), p. 101.

47. Jean-Paul Sartre, *Existentialism*, trans. B. Frechtman (New York: Philosophical Library, 1947), p. 61.

48. Paul L. Holmer, *The Grammar of Faith* (New York: Harper & Row, 1978), p. 133.

49. Joseph Campbell, *Myths to Live By* (New York: Bantam Books, 1973), pp. 88 f.

50. Clifford Geertz, *Islam Observed* (New Haven: Yale University Press, 1968), p. 17.

51. Robert N. Bellah, *Beyond Belief*, p. 227.

52. Talcott Parsons, "Belief, Unbelief, and Disbelief," in Rocco Caporal and Antonio Grumelli, eds. *The Culture of Unbelief* (Berkeley: University of California Press, 1971), p. 226.

### Chapter 3

1. Some of these concerns were raised in Norman Faramelli's "Theology and Social Action: Misuses and Uses of Theological Language," unpublished paper, July, 1978.
2. Cornelis van Peursen, "Man and Reality—The History of Human Thought" in *A Reader in Contemporary Theology*, John Bowden and James Richmond, eds. (Philadelphia: The Westminster Press, 1967), pp. 115-26.
3. von Rad, *Old Testament Theology*, I, p. 121.
4. Jurgen Moltmann, *Hope and Planning*, trans. Margaret Clarkson (New York: Harper & Row, 1971), p. 105.
5. von Rad, *Old Testmanent Theology*, II, p. 350.
6. Rudolf Bultmann, *Primitive Christianity in Its Contemporary Setting*, trans. R. H. Fuller (New York: Living Age Books, 1956), p. 180. Quoted in von Rad, *Old Testament Theology*, II, p. 351, n. 32.
7. H. H. Price, *Belief* (London: George Allen and Unwin, 1969), p. 251.
8. John Hick, *Faith and Knowledge*, 2nd ed. (New York: Macmillan, 1967), p. 122. Quoted in Ian Barbour, *Myths, Models and Paradigms* (New York: Harper & Row, 1974), p. 53.
9. Paul L. Holmer, *The Grammar of Faith* (New York: Harper & Row, 1978), p. 133.
10. Terms used by James M. Gustafson, *Christ and the Moral Life* (New York: Harper & Row, 1968), chapter 7. See also his *Theology and Christian Ethics* (Philadelphia: Pilgrim Press, 1974), pp. 150 f.
11. Dietrich Bonhoeffer, *The Cost of Discipleship*, rev. ed., trans. R. H. Fuller (New York: Macmillan, 1963 [1949]), pp. 63, 67, and 68.
12. *Ibid.*, p. 69.
13. *Ibid.*, pp. 72 f.
14. Bonino, *Christians and Marxists*, p. 40. See also Carl Michalson, *The Rationality of Faith* (New York: Charles Scribner's Sons, 1963), p. 80.
15. Jose Miguez Bonino, *Doing Theology in a Revolutionary Situation* (Philadelphia: Westminster Press, 1975), p. 89.

16. John Baillie, *The Sense of the Presence of God* (New York: Charles Scribner's Sons, 1962), pp. 141, 153.
17. See Paul Holmer, *The Grammar of Faith,* chapters 1 and 2.
18. Leonardo Boff, *Jesus Christ Liberator,* trans. Patrick Hughes (Maryknoll, N.Y.: Orbis Books, 1978), p. 47.
19. *Ibid.,* p. 279.
20. See Gordon Kaufman, *Systematic Theology* (New York: Charles Scribner's Sons, 1968), pp. 27 f.
21. Oscar Cullmann, *Christ and Time,* rev. ed., trans. Floyd V. Filson (London: SCM Press, Ltd., 1951), pp. 19 f.
22. A. N. Whitehead, *Religion in the Making* (New York: The Macmillan Company, 1926), p. 32.
23. *Ibid.,* p. 50.
24. Quoted in Jurgen Moltmann, *Religion, Revolution, and the Future,* trans. M. Douglas Weeks (New York: Charles Scribner's Sons, 1969), p. 65.
25. Karl Barth, *Church Dogmatics,* ed. G. W. Bromiley and T. F. Torrance (Edinburgh: T & T Clark, 1960), III, 3, p. 293.
26. See Rudolf Bultmann's *Jesus Christ and Mythology* (New York: Charles Scribner's Sons, 1958), p. 15.
27. Langdon Gilkey, *Religion and the Scientific Future* (New York: Harper & Row, 1970), pp. 38 ff.
28. Thomas Kuhn, *The Structure of Scientific Revolutions,* 2nd ed. (Chicago: University of Chicago Press, 1970 [1962]).
29. Bultmann, *Jesus Christ and Mythology,* p. 19.
30. See this distinction in John A. T. Robinson, *The Human Face of God* (Philadelphia: The Westminster Press, 1973), p. 21.
31. Herbert W. Richardson, *Toward an American Theology* (New York: Harper & Row, 1967), p. 61.
32. Paul Ricoeur, *The Symbolism of Evil,* trans. Emerson Buchanan (Boston: Beacon Press, 1967), p. 348.
33. David Tracy, *Blessed Rage for Order* (New York: The Seabury Press, 1975), pp. 209 f.
34. John Dominic Crossan, *The Dark Interval: Towards a Theology of Story* (Niles, Illinois: Argus Communications, 1975), p. 59.
35. George Prince, *The Practice of Creativity* (New York: Harper & Row, 1970).
36. C. H. Dodd, *Parables of the Kingdom* (London: Nisbet & Co., 1935), p. 16.
37. Ricoeur, *The Symbolism of Evil,* p. 165.
38. Blaise Pascal, *Pensées,* trans. A. J. Krailsheimer (Baltimore: Penguin Books, 1966), par. 190, p. 86.

39. Howard Thurman, *With Head and Heart* (New York: Harcourt Brace Jovanovich, 1979), p. 21.
40. H. Richard Niebuhr, *The Meaning of Revelation* (New York: Macmillan, 1941), p. 73.
41. The phrase suggested by Hans-Georg Gadamer, *Philosophical Hermeneutics*, trans. and ed. David E. Linge (Berkeley: University of California Press, 1976), pp. xix f.
42. Quoted in Clark C. Abt, *Serious Games* (New York: Viking Press, 1970), p. 12.
43. Albert Outler, *Who Trusts in God: Musings on the Meaning of Providence* (New York: Oxford University Press, 1968), p.29.
44. Wolfhart Pannenberg, *Theology and the Philosophy of Science*, trans. Francis McDonagh (Philadelphia: The Westminster Press, 1976), p. 7; and Emil Brunner, *The Christian Doctrine of God: Dogmatics, Vol. 1*, trans. Olive Wyon (Philadelphia: The Westminster Press, 1950), p. 91.
45. Baillie, *The Sense of the Presence of God*, p. 137.

## Chapter 4

1. See Kaufman, *God the Problem*, pp. 203-25.
2. von Rad, *Old Testament Theology*, I, p. 153.
3. John Hick, *God and the Universe of Faiths* (New York: St. Martin's Press, 1973), pp. 38 ff.
4. A point emphasized in Edward Schillebeeeckx, *Christ: The Experience of Jesus as Lord*, trans. John Bowden (New York: The Seabury Press, 1980), p. 32.
5. The phrase is John Hick's in *God and the Universe of Faiths*, pp. 41 f.
6. Gilkey, *Religion and the Scientific Future*, p. 44.
7. See Kuhn, *The Structures of Scientific Revolutions*, and Barbour, *Myths, Models and Paradigms*.
8. Michael Polanyi, *Personal Knowledge* (Chicago: University of Chicago Press, 1958), pp. 3 ff.
9. *Ibid.*, p. 150.
10. *Ibid.*, p. 151.
11. Barbour, *Myths, Models and Paradigms*, pp. 71-91.
12. Quoted in Daniel Bell, *The Coming of the Post-Industrial Society* (New York: Basic Books, 1973), p. 9.
13. Barbour, *Myths, Models and Paradigms*, pp. 5-6.
14. H. Richard Niebuhr, *The Meaning of Revelation* (New York: Macmillan, 1962), p. 108.
15. *Webster's New Collegiate Dictionary*, S. V. "imagination" (Springfield, Mass.: G. C. Merriam Co., 1953).

16. See Walter Brueggemann, *The Prophetic Imagination* (Philadelphia: Fortress Press, 1978), pp. 66-67.

17. *Ibid.*, p. 45.

18. *Ibid.*, p. 67.

19. Schillebeeckx, *Christ*, p. 50.

20. Juan Luis Segundo, *The Liberation of Theology*, trans. John Drury (Maryknoll, N.Y.: Orbis Books, 1976), pp. 8 f.

21. See James Gustafson, "The Burden of the Ethical: Reflections on Disinterestedness and Involvement," in his *Theology and Christian Ethics* (Philadelphia: Pilgrim Press, 1974), p. 38.

22. Suggested in Richard T. Snyder, "The Politics of Liberation and the Mission of the Church," Ph.D. diss., (Princeton University, 1969), p. 196.

23. Heinrich Ott, "I Believe In," in *Christian Theology: A Case Study Approach*, ed. Robert A. Evans and Thomas D. Parker (New York: Harper & Row, 1976), p. 47.

24. John Macquarrie, *Principles of Christian Theology*, 2nd ed. (New York: Charles Scribner's Sons, 1977), pp. 19-20.

25. Tracy, *Blessed Rage for Order*, p. 243. See the history of the concept in Vazquez, *The Philosophy of Praxis*.

26. Ricoeur, *The Symbolism of Evil*, p. 351.

27. *Ibid.*

28. *The Journal of the Rev. John Wesley, M.A.*, ed. Nehemiah Curnock (London: Epworth Press, 1938), I, p. 442.

29. Martin Luther, *Commentary on the First Twenty-Two Psalms*, vol. 1 of *Luther's Works*, ed. John Nicholas Lenker (Sunbury, Pennsylvania: Lutherans in All Lands Co., 1903), Psalm 5, p. 266.

## Chapter 5

1. The Discipline, p. 46.

2. Adam Clarke, *Memoirs of the Wesley Family, Collected Primarily from Original Documents,* (London: T. Tegg and Son, 1836), II, p. 25.

3. From Wesley's preface to the sermons, in *Sermons on Several Occasions* (New York: Carlton & Phillips, 1854), I, p. 5.

4. *Ibid.*

5. "The Nature, Design, and General Rules of the United Societies," in *The Works of the Rev. John Wesley, A.M.* (London: John Mason, 1856), VIII, p. 260. Hereafter referred to as *Works*.

6. Wesley, "Thoughts upon a Late Phenomenon" (1788), in *Works*, XIII, p. 252 f.

7. The Discipline, p. 46.

8. Sermon on "Original Sin," in *Wesley's Standard Sermons,* ed. Edward H. Sugden, 4th ed. (London: The Epworth Press, 1956), II, p. 216.

9. "Thoughts upon Methodism" (1787), *Works,* XIII, pp. 244 f.

10. Wesley to John Downes, Rector of St. Michael's, in *The Letters of the Rev. John Wesley, A.M.,* ed. John Telford (London: Epworth Press, 1931), IV, p. 333. Hereafter cited as *Letters.*

11. Thomas Jackson, ed., *The Journal of the Rev. Charles Wesley, A.M. . . . to Which are Appended Selections from his Correspondence and Poetry* (London: Wesleyan Methodist Book Room, 1849), I, p. 314.

12. John S. Simon, *John Wesley and the Methodist Societies,* lst ed. (London: Epworth Press, 1923), pp. 101 ff.

13. "To the Editor of 'Lloyd's Evening Post,' " (December 9, 1772), *Letters,* V, pp. 350-54.

14. Richard M. Cameron, *The Rise of Methodism* (New York: Philosophical Library, 1954), pp. 89-90.

15. Wesley to William Wilberforce, *Letters,* VIII, p. 265.

16. "An Earnest Appeal to Men of Reason and Religion," in *The Works of John Wesley,* ed. Gerald R. Cragg (Oxford: At the Clarendon Press, 1975), XI, pp. 66-67.

17. See the letter to the Rev. Freedborn Garrettson (June 26, 1785), *Letters,* VII, pp. 276-77.

18. "Advice to the People Called Methodists" (1745), in *The Works of the Rev. John Wesley, A.M.,* ed. John Emory (New York: J. Emory and B. Waugh, 1831), V, p. 253.

19. Wesley to the Rev. Mr. Venn (June 22, 1763), in *Letters,* V, p. 364.

20. Wesley to Dr. Rutherford (March 28, 1768), *Letters,* V, p. 364.

21. The Discipline, p. 42.

22. *Ibid.,* p. 25.

23. *Ibid.,* pp. 40-71.

24. *Ibid.,* p. 82.

25. *Ibid.,* p. 78.

26. Paul Tillich, *The Courage to Be* (New Haven: Yale University Press, 1952), pp. 32-63.

27. *Ibid.,* pp. 57-63.

28. Gustavo Gutierrez, *Praxis de Liberacion y Fe Christiana,* rev. ed. (San Antonio: Mexican-American Cultural Center, 1976), p. 37.

## Chapter 6

1. *Webster's New Collegiate Dictionary*, S. V. "context."
2. See van Peursen, "Man and Reality—The History of Human Thought," in *A Reader in Contemporary Theology*, p. 125.
3. Terms used by Gustafson, *Christ and the Moral Life*, pp. 240-44.
4. For discussion of these themes, see Mircea Eliade's *Myth and Reality*, trans. Willard R. Trask (Evanston: Harper & Row, 1963), pp. 5 f., 18–30 ff. See also his *Images and Symbols*, trans. Willard R. Trask (New York: Harcourt Brace Jovanovich, 1959), pp. 50-65; and *The Myth of Eternal Return*, trans. Willard Trask (New York: Pantheon Books, 1954).
5. Colin Williams, *Faith in a Secular Age* (New York: Harper & Row, 1966), p. 35.
6. Reinhold Niebuhr, *The Nature and Destiny of Man* (New York: Charles Scribner's Sons, 1941), II, p. 4.
7. See Cullman, *Christ and Time*, pp. 121 ff.
8. Colin Morris, *The Hammer of the Lord* (New York: Abingdon Press, 1973), p. 84.
9. W. H. Auden, "For the Time Being: A Christmas Oratorio" (1945). From *Collected Poems*, ed. Edward Mendelson (New York: Random House, 1976). Used by permission.